PRICELESS MEMORIES

PRICELESS MEMORIES

BOB BARKER

WITH DIGBY DIEHL

CENTER
STREET®

New York   Boston   Nashville

Center Street
Hachette Book Group
237 Park Avenue
New York, NY 10017

Visit our website at www.centerstreet.com

Center Street is a division of Hachette Book Group, Inc.
The Center Street name and logo are registered trademarks
of the Hachette Book Group.

Printed in the United States of America

First Edition: April 2009
10 9 8 7 6 5 4 3 2 1

Library of Congress Cataloging-in-Publication Data
Barker, Bob
  Priceless memories / Bob Barker with Digby Diehl.—1st ed.
    p. cm.
  ISBN 978-1-59995-135-5 (regular edition)
  ISBN 978-1-59995-194-2 (large print edition)
1. Barker, Bob, 1923– 2. Television personalities—
United States—Biography.   I. Diehl, Digby. II. Title.
  PN1992.4.B325A3 2009
  791.4502'8092—dc22
  [B]   2008035208

For my wife, Dorothy Jo,

and my mother, both of whom

loved me and supported me

all the days of their lives

CONTENTS

CONTENTS

PRICELESS
MEMORIES

A Phone Call from Ralph Edwards

If you are fifty years old or younger, I have been on national television your entire life, and I would like to begin this book by telling you how I got there. Hollywood mythology is full of overnight success stories. The urban legend of the discovery of Lana Turner in Schwab's Drugstore is the best-known example, but the entertainment business doesn't really work that way. Before producers are ready to risk a lot of money on you, they demand proof of your ability, your experience, and your professionalism.

In other words, it takes many years of hard work to become an overnight success. On the other hand, I received one unforgettable phone call from Ralph Edwards that truly made possible everything else that happened to me in a long and fortunate life.

• • •

My overnight success began in 1956, nearly seven years after my wife, Dorothy Jo, and I had moved to Hollywood in pursuit of "audience participation host" opportunities for me. At the time, I was doing a weekly radio program on the local CBS station for Southern California Edison. It was called *The Bob Barker Show.* I named it myself. Dorothy Jo produced the show. Southern California Edison was (and is) the electric power company for almost all of the Los Angeles metropolitan area. At the time, Edison maintained what they called Electric Living Centers all over their service area. Essentially, the centers were appliance store showrooms with theater seating—and a microphone.

On the stage were all sorts of ranges, refrigerators, freezers, washers, dryers—anything and everything that used electricity. These were the gleaming modern furnishings of the dream kitchen of the mid-1950s, and the Edison centers offered regular demos in the hope that people would go out and buy new electric appliances for their homes. Edison didn't necessarily care whether you bought Westinghouse or Hotpoint or Maytag, as long as it plugged in. My show featured homemakers who attended these demonstrations and wanted to be on the radio. Dorothy Jo and I would visit two different cities a day, doing a show in each city. We logged a lot of miles traveling out to the rapidly growing suburbs of Los Angeles, including Pomona, San Bernardino, Oxnard, and Ventura—sometimes as far away as Lancaster—to visit these Edison Electric Living Centers and broadcast on KNX radio.

One day shortly after Thanksgiving in 1956, Ralph Edwards was driving his daughters—who were little girls in those days—to an ice-skating lesson. To say that it was my good fortune that he turned on his car radio, and tuned in to *The Bob Barker Show,* is an understatement.

Ralph Edwards was already a broadcasting legend. Beginning as a radio announcer, he went on to become the producer of *This Is Your Life* and a long list of other shows, including, of course, *Truth or Consequences. Truth or Consequences* was Ralph's own creation and was based on a game he played on the family farm as a kid.

I had been a big fan of Ralph Edwards. I used to listen to him when he hosted *Truth or Consequences* on the radio, which he began doing in 1940. He painted such a vivid picture of what was happening that you didn't have to see it, describing things with such flair and detail that you enjoyed every moment of it.

In 1950, they brought *Truth or Consequences* to television, and Ralph hosted that version as well until 1954, when Jack *"Queen for a Day"* Bailey took over. When we came to California, Dorothy Jo and I used to go to watch *Truth or Consequences* live. Ralph built and maintained a tremendous level of excitement. He was almost frenetic in the way he bounded around the stage on *Truth*—not at all as he appeared on *This Is Your Life.*

Occasionally, after playing a joke on a contestant, Ralph would look into the camera and say to the viewers: "Aren't we devils?" People all over the country picked up on it and were saying, "Aren't we devils?" It was the same thing that was to happen with "Come on down" a couple of decades later.

By late 1956, Dorothy Jo and I had a small advertising agency on the Sunset Strip from which we serviced advertisers for *The Bob Barker Show.* And when I say "small," I really mean small. Dorothy Jo and I were it, which meant that when I was out meeting with a client, she was the only one in the office.

"Ralph Edwards called you," she said casually as I walked in the door.

This was nothing to be casual about. "You mean the famous Ralph Edwards?" I asked.

"I guess so," Dorothy Jo replied. "They said 'Ralph Edwards Productions.' "

I started getting excited. "What did he want?" I asked.

"The lady who called said he wants to talk to you."

"Give me that number!"

I sat down immediately and dialed the number.

Ralph came on the line quickly. He said, "I'm calling you because I have a show called *Truth or Consequences* that's going back on TV as a daytime program. I'd like to talk with you about the possibility of you hosting it."

I could hardly believe my ears, but I managed to say, "Yes, sir."

"I was wondering when it would be convenient for you to see me," Ralph said.

I knew that Ralph Edwards Productions was located on Hollywood Boulevard at the corner of Cherokee. I said, "I'll be right over. I can be in your office in fifteen minutes." Perhaps a bit too eager, I started to get up and head for the door—even before I hung up the phone. The cord pulled me up short.

With a smile in his voice, Ralph assured me that it wouldn't be necessary to be there in fifteen minutes. "Bob," he said, "how about tomorrow or the next day?"

I promptly said, "Let's make it tomorrow."

Ralph chuckled as we set up the time for our meeting.

Ralph Edwards Productions had what looked to me like a complete floor, offices in every direction. I told a young lady at a desk near the elevator that I was Bob Barker and that I had an appointment with Mr. Edwards. She asked me, "Ralph or Paul Edwards?"

"Ralph Edwards," I answered.

She picked up a phone, spoke softly for a moment, and said, "Mr. Edwards is expecting you, Mr. Barker. His office is at the end of this hall." She gestured down a long hall.

As I walked down the hall, it seemed as if there were one, two, or sometimes three people busily working away in offices on both sides of the hall.

I thought, "This is one busy place." In the years to come, I learned how right I was.

When I reached Ralph's office, the door was standing open and he was seated at his desk, writing. As I came through the door, he quickly rose and stepped around his huge desk, extending his hand. He said, "Young man, I like the way you do your radio show." As we shook hands, he closed his office door behind me, indicated a chair for me near his desk, and sat down in his own chair.

Of course, Ralph's opening remark that he liked my work on radio did wonders to put me at ease, which was probably exactly what it was intended to do.

Ralph looked even younger—he was forty-two—than he had looked when Dorothy Jo and I had attended his show.

He was wearing a light brown, perfectly fitted single-breasted suit; a white shirt; and a dark brown and yellow tie. I thought he looked every inch the television star and producer that, indeed, he was. His office was spacious and beautifully furnished in brown and beige.

It was just the two of us as Ralph and I sat and talked. He asked some questions about my background and about my experience doing audience participation shows. Apparently, my years of interviewing regular folks in the Edison Electric Living Centers struck him as good preparation for *Truth or Consequences*.

"What did you do before you came to California?" Ralph asked. I told him how I had gotten my start at KTTS in Springfield, Missouri, while I was in college.

"That's exactly how I started in radio when I was at the University of California at Berkeley," Ralph said, and I got the impression that he was pleased we had that in common.

Ralph wanted to know if I was married, and I told him that I had married my high school sweetheart and that my wife produced my radio shows.

"Splendid," he said. "I think we may be onto something here. I'll be in touch."

Incidentally, Paul Edwards was Ralph's older brother. I ended up doing *Truth or Consequences* for Ralph for eighteen years, and not once did Ralph and I argue about money. Paul always handled that.

A few days after my first meeting with Ralph, he called me and said, "I'd like to have you come in and meet some of the people you'd be working with if you did *Truth or Consequences.*" I went back and had a pleasant meeting with them. At the end of the meeting, Ralph said, "I'll be in touch."

When I left I had no idea whether they liked me or not, but shortly thereafter Ralph called and invited me to another meeting. He wanted me to meet some of his representatives and a few others. At that time, MCA had both a talent and a production arm, and they represented Ralph. This time when I got there, I was looking at a roomful of people. Long before the movie *Men in Black,* MCA agents were often described by journalists and industry pundits as "the men in the black suits." When I arrived, I found that their nickname was richly deserved. All three of the men from MCA were clad in practically identical black suits. Also present were executives from NBC, as well as a couple of people from Ralph's production company. And, of course, Ralph himself. We sat and talked some more. At the end of the meeting, Ralph gave me a cheery smile and, like the previous meetings, said, "I'll be in touch."

By this time I was beginning to think, "Barker, can you tolerate many more of these meetings? Can you last through this?" In reality, only a short time had passed since our initial conversation, but the days between meetings seemed to stretch on interminably. I never knew when I'd hear from him again, or *if* I would hear from him again.

It was right around my birthday, December 12, when he

finally called once more. Although the show was to be televised on NBC, Ralph, who had connections with all of the networks, asked me to come down to what is still the oldest CBS television station in the country, on Sunset Boulevard in what is known as Gower Gulch. At the time, it was the nerve center for all of CBS—nationally, locally, and everything else, I guess.

Ralph wanted me to do an audition before a live studio audience. We went over the script, and he told me what he wanted me to do. The show was a segment of *Truth or Consequences*. "Would you like to have somebody do the warm-up for you?" he asked.

"No," I said, "I want to do it myself."

"Bob, would you like to have someone select your contestants?"

"Thanks, Ralph, but no," I responded. "I want to do that, too."

After a warm introduction by a CBS staff announcer, I went onstage. As I went out into the studio audience to select my contestants, I tried not to look at Dorothy Jo. She was seated in the audience and leading the applause, laughing at every word I said, and turning to others who had no idea she was my wife and saying, "Isn't he wonderful?"

I chose my contestants, and we did the show just like a live radio show. As many of you will recall, the basic idea of *Truth or Consequences* was simple. A contestant was asked a less than erudite question, such as "In the days of the Old West, what did it mean when a gunfighter had notches in his gun handle?" The correct answer was "termites." For having failed to answer the question, the contestant had to pay the consequences, which would be a (hopefully) hilarious stunt. The basic idea of the show was simple enough, but the consequences could get complicated, as I shall describe later.

After you have done this for a few years, you know when it's going well, and I knew this afternoon had gone well. I got laughs, and the "consequences" worked.

When I came off the stage, Ralph was waiting in the wings, smiling. I could tell he was pleased. "That went nicely," he said warmly. "If you don't do *Truth or Consequences* for me, I'll have other shows that you might do, but so far as *Truth or Consequences* is concerned . . . I'll be in touch."

This was not what I was hoping to hear. I didn't want to do another show some time in the future. I wanted to do *Truth or Consequences* right now! Some time in the future might never come. I tried to smile my best smile as I said, "Thank you, Mr. Edwards."

I went home worried and frustrated. There seemed to be no end to the number of hoops I would be asked to jump through. Worse yet, Ralph called a few days later and informed me that what we both thought was a successful audition was not really a "television audition" at all, since no one had actually seen me on camera. He asked if I would come down to the old El Capitan Theatre in Hollywood, where they were producing *The Tennessee Ernie Ford Show,* so they could check out my on-camera appearance during a break. I had no idea who they were, but they held my future in their hands.

Joe Landis was one of the pioneering directors of the early days of television, and he was doing Tennessee Ernie's show. As soon as I arrived, they hustled me into makeup and put me in front of a camera to say a few lines with Joe during breaks in the *Tennessee Ernie Ford Show* rehearsal. Ralph was in the

booth with a bunch of other people—and they were all looking intently at me. I was about to find out whether I had a face
made for radio. Finally, Ralph came out of the booth and said
the dreaded words: "I'll be in touch."

I went home despondent. Dorothy Jo commiserated and
tried to console me. I began to wonder if "I'll be in touch" was
one of those Hollywood phrases that was a euphemism for
something more ominous. Can't these people make up their
minds?

A few days later, I got the answer. On December 21, 1956, at
exactly five minutes past noon, Ralph Edwards called me and
told me I was to be the host of *Truth or Consequences*. That
was and is and will always be the most important telephone
call of my professional career. It changed my whole life. That
first national show paved the way for the wonderful half century I have had on television.

At the time, I certainly did not feel like an overnight success,
especially after the ordeal of the last few weeks, but that was
the way many in the industry saw it. Moreover, when I tell that
story, some people shrug and say, "If Ralph Edwards hadn't
called, someone else would have."

Maybe. Maybe not. Maybe I would have spent my entire
life going to Ventura and Oxnard doing the Southern California Edison shows. But Ralph did call, and I signed a contract
shortly thereafter. Ralph made all the difference in my life.

· · ·

Ten days later, we went on the air with our first show. It was
New Year's Eve, December 31, 1956. I will always be grateful
to Ralph for his support and kind words on that show. After

reminding the audience that *Truth or Consequences* was "the granddaddy of audience participation shows," he graciously introduced me as "a young man . . . with one of the brightest futures in television," and over the years he did his best to make that prediction come true.

As I look at it today, that first show is a sweet period piece, a slice of the 1950s right down to the Studebaker prize and the savings bond promotion. With Ralph's glowing introduction of me and the excitement of our special guest, former heavyweight champion Jack Dempsey, we got the show off to a rousing start, and the contestants did the rest.

But that phone call was everything to me. It came after a long string of "I'll be in touch" promises, but it was also the beginning of a bond with Ralph Edwards that lasted a lifetime. He became not only my champion but my mentor and my dear friend. He and his wife, Barbara, became close with Dorothy Jo and me, and really took us under their wing. Every year on December 21, Ralph and I had lunch together, and at five minutes after noon, we drank a toast to our long and enduring friendship. Ralph passed away in 2005, but on that date, at that time, I always pause to thank him.

Truth or Consequences,
My First National Show

The *Truth or Consequences* job that Ralph Edwards gave me was definitely my big break, and it was the foundation of all the wonderful things that came later. Was I lucky? Yes. After all, I had been doing radio shows for years, but I had no television experience. Did I work hard to make the most of the opportunity that Ralph gave me? You bet I did. And I benefited a great deal from Ralph and the very talented staff involved with that show. I was confident that I could do the job. After all, I had done audience participation for so long I was comfortable with the show's format. Also, I knew Ralph Edwards had confidence in me. I had respect for his judgment, so I thought to myself, "You can do this, Barker," and I went out and did it.

However, I didn't make *Truth or Consequences*. If anything,

Truth or Consequences made Bob Barker. At least it made me nationally known and launched my career. It also made me some pretty good money. It's important to remember that the show had already been around for sixteen years—ten on radio and six on television—prior to my arrival. Ralph Edwards was brilliant, a broadcasting legend, and he created the show. Jack Bailey, who was famous as host of *Queen for a Day,* had in fact hosted the show at night for two years just before I got the nod.

I was stepping into an ideal position in four ways. First, the show had a long, successful track record. Second, I was working with incredible talent. They included not only Ralph, but also producer Ed Bailey—who had worked with Ralph for years; announcer/associate producer Charlie Lyon, who left his job as NBC's chief announcer in Chicago to join Ralph's production company; and the unpredictable Milt Larsen, one of our writers, who later went on to start the Magic Castle club in Hollywood. Third, as I look back on this time period—1956 and into the '60s—it was the absolute heyday of television. The advertising industry was booming. The country was prospering, and as the national television audience grew, the major networks were in a perfect position to ride the wave of prosperity and viewership. There was an excitement about television, about broadcasting, about advertising and new products and new technology. We were in Hollywood, the center of entertainment, and this was shaping up to be the golden age of television programming. Finally, Ralph thought that the show played to my strengths. He pointed out that I'd had years of experience ad-libbing and working with audiences. I could choose my own contestants. I could do my own warm-up. He told me that he was sure I would be completely comfortable doing *Truth or Consequences*. Ralph said, "*T or C* is a good fit for you and you are a good fit for the show." All of this was music to my ears.

Make no mistake: it was a major break and an extraordinary opportunity for me. I did go on to have a fabulous eighteen-year run with *Truth or Consequences*. But when I started, I was hired on a four-week trial basis, and while Ralph was confidently in my corner, I had no guarantees that I would be retained beyond that initial probationary period.

I told you that Dorothy Jo was in the audience for my audition. Well, she was right there laughing it up for me at my early shows, too. I could always depend upon Dorothy Jo to help in every way possible.

As I have mentioned, my first show was December 31, 1956. We did the show live back in those days in the NBC studio at the corner of Sunset and Vine. The reason for that four-week clause in my contract, I learned later, was that out of eleven people voting in the original hiring meeting, I got only one vote. But I got the right one, Ralph Edwards. He told them, "This guy is your man. You give him four weeks and see if you don't agree."

During that first show, I said to Ralph on air, "Following you and Jack Bailey, I feel like I'm hitting after Babe Ruth and Lou Gehrig." Ralph said, "Well, we've got to bring along the Mantles and the DiMaggios." He was very kind. I'll never forget that.

I was definitely nervous backstage before the show. My heart was beating so fast that I thought I might have a heart attack before I ever got out there. But on the show itself, I wasn't nervous. The staff and crew did everything possible to make me feel at home, and the show went well.

We had Jack Dempsey, the former heavyweight boxing champion, on the first show. He was a real gentleman. Jack was much bigger than I had expected. I had read that he was a relatively small heavyweight. But *small* was not a word I would associate with him. His hands were huge. When I shook hands with him it seemed as if his hand covered mine all the way up to the elbow. We also gave away a Studebaker, a sporty five-seater called the Seahawk. That was a huge prize back then.

Years later, I remember we had another boxing champion, Joe Louis, on *T or C*. This was long after he had been champion and he was retired. He was a very nice fellow, soft-spoken but outgoing, and a good conversationalist. I interviewed him at some length, and I asked him, "Who was your toughest opponent?" When he answered, "The IRS," everyone in the audience knew exactly what he meant. Poor old Joe, they knocked him around a bit.

• • •

The tremendous popularity of *Truth or Consequences* over the years was a result of the show's humor, the games and practical jokes, and the audience participation. We also had many celebrity guests, but the prizes added to the excitement. Many of the products given away were new additions to the American home. We gave away refrigerators, washers, dryers, and other large home appliances. Even the small gifts, like coffee percolators, were new products that advertisers, sponsors, and consumers were all excited about.

During my first seven years on *T or C,* we would sometimes

tape at the El Capitan Theatre. We were back and forth between there and the studio at Sunset and Vine. Talk about landmark locations: Sunset and Vine and the El Capitan Theatre! I'll never forget doing the show live at the El Capitan Theatre at 8:00 a.m. Can you imagine coming to *Truth or Consequences* at 8:00 a.m.? Remarkably, we were packed every day. We filled the place. On the marquee it said, "Free donuts and Bob Barker." When I finished my four-week probation and they hired me on long term, I had the sign changed to "Bob Barker and free donuts." I told them, "I'm not going to be billed under the donuts any longer."

Doing *Truth or Consequences* at the El Capitan Theatre was no problem whatsoever. As I wrote earlier, *The Tennessee Ernie Ford Show* was taping there regularly, so it was well lighted for television and the sound system was excellent. We just moved our regular set to the El Capitan stage, and with our regular technicians and crew, we were ready to get it on.

But we were happiest in Studio D at the NBC Studios at Sunset and Vine. At that time, I think Studio D was the best studio in Hollywood for audience participation. The seats were banked up from stage level so every person in the audience could see everything that happened on stage perfectly. Folks in the first few rows were at risk when we started throwing the lemon meringue pies for which *T or C* was famous. And access to the audience from the stage was completely unimpeded. There wasn't even a step. The aisle began right at stage level, which was very convenient when we did a consequence that required me to go into the audience.

If I sound as if I was fond of Studio D, I assure you that I was. So much so, in fact, that when the old NBC studio was demolished, Charlie Lyon saved the Studio D flashing red ON THE AIR sign as a gift for me and I hung it over the bar in my home.

When we taped in Studio D, we could do things out on the street, too. We used hidden cameras to play jokes on people walking by the studio. We were surrounded by traffic and tourists. We had a big sign outside that said TRUTH OR CONSEQUENCES, and many tourists decided on the spot to come in and watch the show. But when the network decided that we were going to color from black and white, they moved us to the new studios in Burbank.

We really did have a lot of firsts on *T or C*. We were one of the first shows to broadcast in color—and we were one of the first shows to tape in Burbank. All shows would tape occasionally, but we were the first national television show to tape on a regular schedule. Later on, we were the first show to produce directly for syndication with the Metromedia television network. Before that time, all of the shows in syndication had been reruns.

Although it is difficult to imagine now, in 1964 the NBC studio in Burbank was literally in the middle of a field. We hated it. We lost all of the foot traffic we had in Hollywood, so there were no walk-ins. And worse yet, you couldn't play jokes on people walking by—because nobody walked by. If you wanted to come to the show, you had to take the bus or drive to Burbank. Tourists had trouble even finding Burbank.

• • •

On a happier note, one of the best aspects of *Truth or Consequences* was that it was always fresh. We did three consequences a day, and each one was different and self-contained. We produced five shows a week. I've always said I was lucky to get the *Truth or Consequences* job early in my career because I learned so much doing it and it prepared me so well for other things I did in broadcasting. Each consequence was like a drama. You start with a question, reveal the consequence, carefully build toward the climax, and then pay it off with a hilarious finish. Every consequence was a learning experience, particularly during my first few years on the show.

I believe many people never get the opportunity to demonstrate their sense of humor. One of the great parts of my job as host was to bring out this humor in people and to enjoy it. That was one of the rewards of my work—seeing people having fun and laughing uproariously, not just at others, but at themselves.

Choosing contestants was like casting a play or a movie. I knew what the act or stunt required, and I tried to find the best person in the audience to play the role. I went through the audience and asked who wanted to play *Truth or Consequences*. Practically all of the people in the audience raised their hands. Then I picked one and asked him or her to stand up. When you stand up, you're no longer part of the audience, you're an individual now, and all eyes are on you. I wanted to see how potential contestants were going to react and how the audience was going to react to them. Some people have this wonderful thing: as soon as they stand up everybody loves them. I'd say, "What's your name?" And he'd just say, "Fred Jones," and right away people loved him. Audiences react that way to certain people. I selected contestants very carefully, based on the potential contestant's reactions, the audience's reactions, and my knowledge of what the consequence involved.

For example, I might choose a younger man rather than an older man because the consequence involved something physical. Many acts required couples, so I looked for married folks who were there together. Other times, I might look for older women or men or someone middle-aged. And, of course, we had children on from time to time. On *T or C,* I almost always worked with contestants who were not preselected or coached. Almost all of the contestants were picked by me right out of the studio audience, and I preferred it that way. I prefer to work with unrehearsed people right out of the audience because that spontaneity is so vital. I think that spontaneous reaction is a major part of the success of both *Truth or Consequences* and *The Price Is Right.* So many memorable comic moments are unscripted—in fact, those are the best kind.

The contestants didn't have a week to worry about being on television. They hadn't had their hair done or selected their best dress. They weren't even made up. They had their normal street makeup on, if they were women, and there they were: suddenly on television—just like the people at home who were watching them and identifying with them.

Above, I noted that "I almost always worked with contestants who were not preselected" because at times we used what we called "set-up contestants." These might be a husband who helped us to play a joke on his wife or a woman who would help us play a joke on her club—that sort of thing.

Back then, it was all about creating spontaneous entertainment with ordinary people. I listened to the successful hosts on radio. Tom Brenneman used to do a show called *Breakfast in Hollywood* on Vine Street in a little restaurant. He'd take a microphone and just go from table to table, talking with the people eating there. If one group of people was lively or entertaining, he'd stay with them; if not, he'd move on to the next table. It was fun and interesting. You could never sell a show like that today. It requires experience to do pure audience participation, and today there is almost no place where you can get that experience.

Years ago, almost every radio station—large or small—originated at least a few shows that required the host to talk with ordinary people. That is no longer true, so young people have no place to develop their skills. No matter how much natural talent you have for audience participation, there is no substitute for experience. Ralph and I grew up in a different world. Ralph was a master host, one of the very best, and he knew that imitation might be the highest form of flattery, but imitation was not the way to go if you were hosting a television show.

Before I did *Truth or Consequences* for the first time, Ralph told me, "Bob, you are the star of this show now. Go out there and do it your way. Don't imitate me or anyone else. Do it Bob Barker's way."

I think Ralph's advice to me was right on. I believe in it so much that I have repeated it to every young host who has ever asked me for advice: "Do it your way." Don't forget that Frank Sinatra even put it to music!

In the early days of *Truth or Consequences,* someone told me: "You've got to remember you're playing to a lady who's in front of an ironing board, somewhere in the room with her is a baby crying, with one hand she's trying to iron and the other hand she has on the TV dial. You have to capture her attention and entertain her or she's going to turn that dial!"

That's what you always have to remember. When you are doing the show, you are talking to that person at home. If you ignore that fact, you're in trouble. On *Truth or Consequences* we had a camera for me to speak directly to the home audience. Every once in a while, when I was talking to a contestant, I turned to look directly into that camera and spoke to the audience at home. That was important. Of course, you want the studio audience to be a part of it from the moment the show begins to the moment it ends. You want to keep them completely involved—just gather them in and cradle them—but you never want to forget the fact that the person at home is watching.

* * *

On *Truth,* I always made sure that nobody answered the question correctly. I had chosen the contestants because they were just right for the consequences, and I didn't want to lose them. I made certain that the questions and answers were so comically crazy that there was almost no chance of a correct answer. For example:

Q: What did one eye say to the other eye?
A: Just between us, something smells.

Q: Which side of a duck has the most feathers?
A: The outside.

Q: What do snakes do after they have a fight?
A: They hiss and make up.

If someone did answer a question, I would discover that it was a two-part question. Only once in all of the years that I hosted *T or C* did a contestant answer the second part of a question. Of course, I immediately made that one a three-part question. No one ever got away!

The production team on *Truth or Consequences* was like a well-oiled machine, and we had fun doing the show. The writers were fantastic. Some of the stunts and games they came up with were amazing. One of the most popular acts was the reunions. One moment the audience was howling at one of the consequences, and the next moment we had one of these reunions with a soldier and his mother, or long-lost brothers, or someone like that. Frequently, everyone, sometimes including the production staff, was in tears.

One reunion I will never forget. We had these two Italian sisters on the show who had not seen each other for thirty years. One lived in California, in the San Fernando Valley, and the other one still lived in Italy. We had the sister from Italy flown in, and we were going to surprise the sister who lived in the Valley. I got the sister who lived here in California on the stage, and when her Italian sister walked out from the wings, it was too much for her. Her mouth dropped open and she fainted dead away. Out cold.

It was toward the end of the show, and we couldn't revive her. I had to sign off with two or three members of the staff still over her trying to wake her up. We decided to have the sisters back the next day so we could show our audience that the "victim" of the reunion had recovered. So the next day, I opened the show standing onstage with the sister from the Valley—the one who fainted—and I tell the audience: "You remember yesterday . . . Well, see, she's okay, we revived her and everything is fine. Let's bring out her sister again." And when the sister from Italy walks onstage—*boom*—the Valley sister faints again. This time we just hauled her off. No more explanations!

The reunions were such a popular feature of the show that they spawned *This Is Your Life,* which ran on NBC for eight years. Charlie Lyon, an associate producer as well as our announcer, orchestrated all the reunions. His brother was a diplomat in the State Department, and I could see why. Charlie had the same genes. He was a perfect gentleman. We called him the Rembrandt of Reunions because he arranged so many of them so well.

• • •

My wife, Dorothy Jo, was a frequent and popular visitor to the show. Sometimes her appearance was my idea; more often the writers would suggest it. Whenever they were in a dry spell and it was getting down to the time they had to come up with something, they'd say, "Let's do a Dorothy Jo act." I'd say fine, and we'd bring her back to save the day.

I will never forget our first Dorothy Jo consequence. It set the pace for all of those that followed. I selected two ladies from the studio audience whose assignment would be to question three women and choose the one who was Mrs. Bob Barker.

After sending these two ladies backstage, I chose two more ladies from the studio audience who would join Dorothy Jo and claim to be my wife. For these roles, I selected two ladies who impressed me as being clever, witty, and able to think fast in an ad-lib situation. One of these phony wives from the audience proved to be fast on her feet beyond my wildest expectations. Responding to questions during the playing of the game, she accused me of continually complaining about her cooking, spending every free moment on the golf course, and drinking so many martinis that I couldn't carry on a conversation after eight thirty in the evening.

Of course, the audience loved every word of it. The studio rocked with laughter. But, as usual, Dorothy Jo had the last laugh. She looked up at me and sweetly said, "Honey, this lady has you pegged right down the line."

The two interrogators correctly chose Dorothy Jo as Mrs. Bob Barker.

My mother was on *Truth or Consequences* occasionally. In fact, the producers even played a prank on me with my mother. When my mother was still living in Missouri, they had her flown out here to surprise me. I had selected a lady from the audience and I expected her to be brought around on a turntable. But when the turntable came around, there was my own mother smiling at me! I was blown away. Totally surprised. I behaved like a typical contestant. I turned my back on the camera and did everything wrong. I'll never forget it. They had really surprised me.

We even had my basset hound on the show. Early in my career, I had been mistakenly called Mr. Baker so many times that I named my pet basset hound Mr. Baker. He would come on the show just to say hello, and the audience loved him. Still to this day, I'll be in a pet store or somewhere like that, and someone will say, "Oh, I used to watch you on *Truth or Consequences,* and I loved your dog." That's the lasting impression animals make.

. . .

We also did a lot of outdoor stunts and jokes on the show. There was an office building next to the NBC studio at Sunset and Vine. It was about three stories, I guess. One day we hung a piano up there, coming out of the third-floor window on a cable. Then we had one of our guys on the street, holding a rope. We fixed it so it appeared he was holding up the piano by holding the rope—but of course he wasn't. A young man came walking down Vine, and our man called out to him, asking him to help him for just one minute. Our man says, "Please, sir, I'm holding that piano up there, and it's very expensive. Would you please just hold it for one moment while I go into the building for my helper? But for goodness sake, don't drop it. Don't leave. Hold that piano."

The pedestrian said, "Sure." So he's holding the rope, and then there's a little jerk on the rope, and the piano kind of moves, and all of a sudden the whole thing breaks off and the piano comes crashing down to the street. The fellow dropped the rope and took off running up Vine Street as fast as he could go. I'm calling out on a speaker to him, "Hey, it's Bob Barker. You're on *Truth or Consequences*." But he just kept running and running. We never caught him or located him later, so we couldn't give him his prize. More's the pity, but the audience loved it.

. . .

We did another stunt outside Grauman's Chinese Theatre that played splendidly. We had a small truck parked in front of the theater, in the back of which was a cage filled with straw and a sizable chimpanzee. Only it wasn't a chimpanzee. It was actually a fellow named Janos Prohaska, and he could convince you that you were with a chimp when he was in costume. He was amazing. Anyway, he's in the cage, and Milt Larsen, one of our writers, was up there on the back of the truck. He held the cage door closed and waited for the right-looking guy to come by, someone perfect for the joke. Here came a man, a big broad-shouldered fellow, who we found out later had played professional football for the Los Angeles Dons. Milt says to the guy, "Excuse me, sir, would you help me for a moment? I have my chimpanzee in here, and this lock isn't working properly. I have to go into the theater to get my tools. Would you just hold the door shut for me for a couple of moments?"

The man says yes, he'd be happy to. So the former football player gets up there and holds the cage door, and Milt says thank you and goes into the theater. There used to be a restaurant next to Grauman's, and that's where I was lying down beside our hidden camera. The cameraman and I are watching this gag unfold. We had hidden microphones all over the place. The chimp appeared to be over in a corner, asleep, but after Milt goes into the theater, the chimp wakes up and starts throwing a little straw around the cage. Now this big virile man holding the cage door starts talking baby talk to the chimp. "That's all right, baby. Daddy will be right back. Just relax, baby, it's all right."

And the chimp moves around a little more and moves toward the door.

The baby talk continues. "It's all right, baby. Back up, baby. Get back, baby. Daddy will be right back."

He's still baby talking to the chimp when all of a sudden

the chimp grabs the cage door and flings it open. Now the guy has dropped the baby talk, and he's yelling, "Back, you son of a [*bleep*]. Back, you [*bleep*]! Down!" And the chimp keeps after him, and now the man runs into the theater with the chimp chasing him, and he's yelling the whole time, "Leave me alone, you [*bleep*]. Down! Back, you son of a [*bleep*]! Don't touch me!" Bleep this and bleep that, and you bleepedy bleep bleep!

I was laughing so hard I couldn't even get up off the floor. We called it our bleep consequence. We played it on the air just like it happened—with all of the bleeps.

So Milt comes out and tells him it's all right. It's not really a chimp. It's Janos Prohaska pretending to be a chimp. And I'm still laughing on the floor, but I finally crawl out of the hiding spot and go up to this fellow, who's not in a good mood. I said, "I'm Bob Barker and you are on *Truth or Consequences*."

He says, "Yes, I know who you are."

And then I tell him what fun the stunt has been, and how we have a great prize for him. I tell him we have a fancy new billiards table for him.

He looks right at me and says, "What the [*bleep*] am I going to do with that?"

It was the perfect end to the bleep consequence.

On another show we invited a bunch of kids who played in Little League baseball to be in the audience. They were all nine- or ten-year-old boys. Then we got two girls; maybe they were fourteen or fifteen. One girl was a professional softball pitcher. She could throw a softball like lightning. And the other girl, her sister, who was also a professional, was her catcher. We planted these girls in the audience, but not together, and pretended to the boys that we just picked them out randomly from the audience. I said something like "How about you, young lady, would you like to play? Yes? Come on." I picked a few of the boys from the Little League group and said, "Let's have a game."

I told them: "We're going to play softball. You three guys are going to hit, and you, young lady, you be the catcher. And you, would you be the pitcher, please?"

She goes all the way across the stage. And the boys are licking their chops, saying, "Oh, this is going to be fun." I put a particularly eager young fellow up to hit, and this professional pitcher throws that ball so fast past him, he doesn't twitch a muscle.

"Why didn't you swing at it?" I asked.

He says, "That's a phony ball."

The audience roared with laughter.

"That's not a phony ball," I said, and I took it from the catcher. "Look at this, that's not a phony ball."

"Well then, she's got a phony arm," he said, and the audience howled even louder.

*   *   *

Things didn't always go as planned on *Truth or Consequences*. That was part of the fun of the show. We had all kinds of things go wrong, but I just made the best of it, and the show rolled on. We had props that didn't work. We had camera or microphone malfunctions. Sometimes a guest would react unexpectedly. But even when acts didn't come off smoothly, there was always humor in them, and the audience seemed to love it. We'd have things that would fail miserably, but when they did, frequently I could make it amusing. Besides, people loved to see me standing there with egg on my face.

. . .

There were so many details involved with reunions that they occasionally went awry. For one, we had a deserving young marine flown home from Korea to surprise his wife. One of his wife's friends arranged to have her sitting on a bench in front of our studio at Sunset and Vine, and on cue from us, a city bus (which we rented for the day) was supposed to pull up in front of the bench and the marine was going to step off the bus and take his wife into his arms.

I described exactly what we had planned to our studio audience and viewers. I emphasized what a fine record the marine had and how courageous the young wife had been during the months that she and the children had anxiously awaited his return. I built to the boiling point the anticipation for that glorious moment when husband and wife would be reunited. And then I went into a commercial.

After the commercial, I did a quick review to make sure that every viewer realized how fortunate he or she was to share this moment with this loving husband and wife. Then, at the exact time, to the second, that we had agreed for the bus to arrive on the scene, I cut to our outside camera.

The marine and his wife were sitting on the bus stop bench chatting. The bus had arrived during the commercial. I looked into the camera and said, "It must have been a great reunion. I wish we could have seen it."

Some time later, after many flawless successes, another reunion went sour. This one was to be more dramatic than even the soap opera fare. This time we were reuniting a fine young sailor and his dear old mother.

The sailor's sister brought their mother to the NBC studio in Burbank. The mother thought that they were to be part of a group touring the facility. The sister knew that the group consisted of folks I took out of our *T or C* audience to help our little caper—for which, of course, each would receive a prize.

This was the plan: As the tour group arrived onstage, every light in the studio was to go out except for one powerful spotlight casting a pool of light directly on center stage. As you might have guessed, on cue, the sailor was to step into the pool of light, the mother would rush to her beloved son, the sister would join them, and familial happiness would reign. But all of this was not to be the case. We have all had really bad experiences with the best-laid plans, haven't we?

As usual, I did my breathless buildup for the momentous moment. I would like to think that I had the folks in our studio on the edges of their seats—the folks at home, too, if they were seated when I received the signal that the tour group was stepping through the door. I asked the lighting man to douse the lights.

He more than cooperated. He shut down every light in the place, including the all-important spotlight. The entire studio was in total darkness, and it stayed that way for about two minutes, during which I had to keep talking in a desperate effort to keep viewers from thinking NBC had gone off the air—and to keep them from changing channels!

What did I say? I have no idea. But I did get a letter from a lady who wrote, "Bob, you do your best work in the dark."

By the way, eventually we got the sailor and his mother together and everyone lived happily ever after.

. . .

There were many memorable moments on *Truth or Consequences*. I have a treasure chest of memories of all the fun we had doing that show. Of course, it was special to meet all the celebrity guests we had. But the average-person guests, the noncelebrities, were just as memorable.

Everyone knows I'm an animal lover, and I will tell you about another reunion featuring a boy and his dog that touched me as deeply as any reunion we ever did. We heard about a sailor who was stationed in Florida who had received orders to come out here to one of the naval bases around Los Angeles. He was married and had a little son, about nine or ten years old. The son had a basset hound, but he didn't have the money to move the dog. So they left the dog with a friend in Florida, and they came out to California. The boy got a job delivering papers so he could save up enough money to get his dog out here. But it was going slowly. We heard about this and of course had the dog flown out here, and somehow we arranged to get the boy to the show and have him end up talking with me in the hallway, where we had a hidden camera and a hidden microphone. The boy didn't know we were on the air. During our conversation he mentioned his dog. He said he was working to save money and bring him out here. I said, "You really love that dog, don't you?"

And he said, "Oh, yes, I do." The dog's name was Bo.

At that moment, one of our people from the show comes down the hallway, and he's leading Bo on a leash. The boy looks up at the dog, and says: "That looks like Bo!"

And I said, "That is Bo."

And he just bolted for the dog. He hugged him and kissed him and hugged him some more. It was a precious moment. I was so touched I could hardly speak. I had tears in my eyes. And I wasn't the only one. The cameramen were all crying, and later I mentioned it to the director, and he said, "Not only you, but the agency reps in the booth had tears in their eyes, and that doesn't happen often." That is one of the most touching moments we ever had.

I had thirty-five great years on *The Price Is Right,* but *Truth or Consequences* will always hold a special place in my heart for many reasons. It was my first national television job; I had the opportunity to work with one of my heroes, Ralph Edwards; and Dorothy Jo and I began to enjoy more financial security. We didn't change our lifestyle much, but the opportunity to do the show was a fulfillment of a dream we had had. It was also a glorious pioneering time in television, and so much of the country was energized and united by television. The whole entertainment industry was thriving. We were living in Hollywood, working in Hollywood, and I was having fun doing what I loved to do. *Truth or Consequences* was a fun-filled, richly rewarding eighteen-year ride for me. I'll always cherish those early years.

I was delighted to have Ralph's son, Gary Edwards, who was a little boy when I went to work for his father, in the front row five decades later, cheering me on as I taped my last *The Price Is Right* on June 6, 2007.

I Go to Work for
Mark Goodson, Too

If the 1950s were the golden age of television, then the 1970s were the silver age, because that's when we relaunched *The Price Is Right* daytime television show, which became a huge success that exceeded all of our expectations. *The Price Is Right* had been a successful television show for years before I ever became involved with it, but it had been off the air for eight years. We believed we were going to have a successful show, but no one could have predicted that I would go on to host the show for thirty-five years and that the program would become a landmark ratings star and an institution of daytime television history. Unless your hair is becoming gray and you have discovered a few wrinkles, *The Price Is Right* is probably the show for which you remember me. From the very beginning, I loved it and never stopped loving it.

. . .

To put the show in historical perspective, we need to go back to 1971. I had been doing *Truth or Consequences* on television since 1956. That's fifteen years of hosting a national audience participation show. Before that, I had done live radio shows for six years with similar spontaneous entertainment formats. That is what I did. That is what I always did. Even before the Edison shows, I did shows from grocery stores, drugstores, theaters, and parks. I did man-on-the-street shows, and I did shows from department stores and hardware stores. I was always improvising, making conversation, and creating spontaneous entertainment with unrehearsed people. I didn't act. I didn't sing. I didn't dance. I didn't tell jokes. But I was experienced at audience participation. Some people like playing the saxophone. I liked doing audience participation shows.

When I started in this business, many of the great hosts were doing audience participation shows. Art Linkletter had his shows. Ralph Edwards was brilliant on his. Jack Bailey of *Queen for a Day* was another great one. I got my first radio show in Missouri when I was twenty-one years old, and it was the same kind of show I would go on doing until I retired at eighty-four. I enjoyed it when I was young, and I enjoyed it just as much when I became not so young.

Mark Goodson, one of the all-time great game show minds, had created *The Price Is Right* and put it on NBC back in 1956. The original host was Bill Cullen, and the show ran on NBC until 1963. ABC actually picked up the program briefly, but *Price* went off the air in 1965. Mark Goodson had a great talent for games and television. He was what is called a game show packager. A game show packager assembles all of the elements of the show—the idea for the show, host, cast, producer, director, staff—and, probably the most important of all, he sells the show to a network or in syndication. He puts the whole package together.

Mark Goodson and Ralph Edwards were two of the best in the business. Goodson also developed *What's My Line?*, *To Tell the Truth*, and *I've Got a Secret*. He had great instincts. Both of them were savvy professionals.

Game shows take a lot of time to develop—tinkering with ideas, coming up with the right format, and just the right combination of chance, entertainment, and novelty. And when the shows are a success, they can be extremely lucrative. By their very nature, game shows are a huge profit center for the networks. They are relatively inexpensive to produce, and they can bring in substantial advertising revenue. For decades, daytime game show profits helped to fund the networks' more expensive prime-time mistakes. The creators and men behind these shows were shrewd, whip smart, and financially astute businessmen. Many of them, like Mark Goodson and his partner Bill Todman, became enormously wealthy. Merv Griffin was another fellow, who, in addition to everything else he did, created *Jeopardy!* and *Wheel of Fortune*. He made a fortune, too.

I have always said that game shows within the television industry are like the stock market. There are times when they are enormously popular. Several shows within the genre will flourish, and programmers will be flooding the market with new game shows. Then there are times when game shows slump, popularity wanes, and the networks pull back. But like the stock market, after a while, the game shows surge back in popularity.

Goodson had talked to me at one time about doing another show called *Beat the Clock* for syndication. For me that was a problem because I was doing *Truth or Consequences* in syndication and my contract stipulated that I could not do another syndicated show. I didn't want to leave *Truth* and I couldn't do both, so Mark and I couldn't get together on *Beat the Clock*.

But a few years later, in 1972, Mark contacted me about doing a network show. Contractually there would not be a problem—although my contract for *T or C* prohibited me from doing another syndicated program, I could do a network show. Mark wanted to bring back *The Price Is Right* on CBS, and he wanted me as the host. We met, and he told me about his ideas for various games he wanted to do on the show and how he wanted to structure the format. Mark told me he thought I would be perfect for the show and asked me if I was interested. I thought it was a great idea. After all, it was the kind of audience participation show I had been doing all my life, and I did not have to leave *Truth or Consequences*.

Before *The Price Is Right* came back on the air, audience participation shows had lost some of their luster. In fact, CBS had not had a game show on the network for four years. However, both Mark Goodson and I were confident that *The New Price Is Right,* as it was called then, would be very successful. Mark had fine-tuned the show to make it much faster moving, more audience friendly, and more dynamic all around. Also, the show was designed to give me every opportunity to interact with the contestants and the studio audience. It would have the feel of a live event—with more games, more variety, and, of course, bigger prizes.

It was still a gamble, I suppose, but those of us involved thought we had a winning formula. I started doing *The Price Is Right* on September 4, 1972. The longest and most rewarding ride of my career was under way.

As it turned out, I did leave *Truth or Consequences* about three years later, but for the first three years that I was on *Price*—1972 through 1974—I did both shows. I was on a half hour a day with *Price,* and a half hour every night with *Truth.* By 1975, we had taped enough *Truth* shows for a year of syndication. These shows had been seen in only four markets. In a smart move, they just stopped production, used the backlog, and made nothing but money for a year with no production costs. During that year, *Price* went from its half-hour format to a full hour.

Truth or Consequences wanted me to do the show again, but Sol Leon, a legendary agent with the William Morris Agency who was representing me at the time, advised me not to do it. He said that with an hour in the daytime and a half hour at night I'd be overexposed. I took his advice, and we passed on continuing with *Truth or Consequences.* Also, my decision was influenced by the fact that some of the people with whom I had worked were gone, the most important one being Ed Bailey, the producer. Bobby Lauher, one of my favorite writers on the show, had died as well, and Charlie Lyon, a dear friend, had retired.

• • •

Mark Goodson was a smart businessman, a generous soul, and the one who brought me to *The Price Is Right*. I did hear a few years later, however, that Mark wasn't the only one who wanted me to do *The Price Is Right*. Bud Grant, who later went on to become a legendary television executive, was more instrumental in orchestrating the whole deal than I realized. At the time, Bud Grant was head of daytime television at CBS. He had been the assistant to the director of daytime at NBC when I had hosted *Truth*. By this time he was head of daytime at CBS, and he had told Mark Goodson that he would buy *The Price Is Right* for CBS if Mark could get me to host it. Mark was always generous with me, but if I had known that he had to have me host the show in order for Bud to buy it, Mark would have been even more generous with me. I told him that, too. We laughed about it.

In fact, I remember that Bud Grant made a pitch to me when I was having some last-minute doubts. He said, "You come over here and do *Price* on CBS, and good things are going to come of it." I'll never forget that because after he bought *Price*, a bit of time passed and he was moved from head of daytime to head of all entertainment on CBS. When I saw him, I said, "Congratulations, Bud. I remember when you told me that if I came over to CBS good things would happen. I didn't understand at the time that these would be 'good things' for Bud Grant. I assumed they would be for Bob Barker." I kidded him about that for years.

But he deserved all his success. Bud Grant knew daytime. He didn't just buy *Price*, he also bought Jack Barry's *The Joker's Wild* and *Gambit* with Wink Martindale. Both shows debuted the same day that *Price* did, and all three shows were hits.

Bud also bought *The Young and the Restless* and *The Bold and the Beautiful,* both of which are still thriving on CBS. In fact, CBS has been number one in daytime ratings for twenty years, thanks in no small part to Bud Grant's purchases and scheduling. He really knew daytime, particularly game shows.

Speaking of ratings, *The Price Is Right* was a smash from day one. We never had a ratings problem. That's a testimony to the energy, the chemistry, and the enthusiasm that was so much a part of the show. It was electric, in fact. There was terrific energy in the studio when we went on the air, and it never let up. There are shows that actually have to buy audiences, but our problem was fitting people in. We had lines around the building, and some people sleeping out there.

● ● ●

But let me get back to the early days of *The Price Is Right.* I want to explain why I think the show was so successful. First, these types of shows were not originally called game shows, they were called audience participation shows, and that's the key element of them. It was always the spontaneous nature of the entertainment, the guests' reactions, the unscripted moments, the enthusiasm, the humor, and the personalities of average people getting excited and having fun. When people asked me how I made a living, I told them I made a living creating spontaneous entertainment with unrehearsed contestants.

I never wanted contestants who were chosen two weeks in advance; taught a game; told what to say, how to smile, and how to react. I was not interested in that. I wanted to talk with people who are surprised they're suddenly on television—totally natural. They might be standing there in a coat and tie or in shorts and sandals with a sunburned nose, but they're natural. The personalities of the contestants were the lifeblood of the show. People in the audience would root for the contestants, and the viewers would be rooting for them, too. Everyone entered into the fun. People at home enjoy it vicariously. They picture themselves there at the show. They may be in the middle of Nebraska, but they'd love to be out in Hollywood winning a car.

It is always about the people. The host and the games and the prizes are all-important, but on *TPIR* it has always been the contestants and the audience who provide the energy, the laughs, and the opportunity to create the beautiful and hilarious moments that keep bringing people back for more. People ask me what makes a good contestant. I always say someone who behaves naturally. For *Price,* some people think they have to jump around and scream or they won't get on the show. They try to do that, but if it's phony, it won't work. If that is not your natural way, then you are not going to come off well trying to do it. But if that is your natural way, it will happen. I have had people, taciturn individuals, who were hilarious. They were great fun. And if you behave naturally and are reasonably outgoing when you are standing in line at *Price,* you have a chance to get on the show. If you are too introverted, it is not going to work; but if you try too hard, it's not going to work either. Just be natural. That's the way to be a good contestant.

I didn't select my own contestants on *Price.* Originally, we had one of the producers do it, and eventually we had contestant coordinators do it. We probably had over the years half a dozen people doing it. But all of them knew I wanted people with whom I could have fun. Our contestant coordinators went out into the line outside before the show and talked to people. They made their selections following my guidelines, but I never knew who was going to be on the show and the people chosen to be contestants didn't know either. They didn't know until their name was called to "Come on down!" That's how we got those wonderful reactions of joy.

Another facet of *Price*'s success is that the show always had a live feel. This was intentional, and it was a big part of the show's energy and appeal. As I've said, my background was in live entertainment, on both radio and television, so that's what I felt comfortable in and that's the environment and attitude I wanted to foster. That's what I had done all over Southern California on radio shows with Dorothy Jo and on *Truth or Consequences*.

• • •

I always brought the shows out on time. In other words, I did them in time to match the allotted length of the show. This assured that the broadcast had a live feel, which everyone loved. Beyond that, I also wanted to decide what went on the air. I didn't want somebody to edit the show and decide that this goes and this stays. I didn't want someone else deciding what's funny about the show. I know what's funny. I did it. If you do it live to time, that's it. What you see is what you get. So that's what I did. If something went wrong, you covered, one way or the other. If you do it live to time, it also has that consistent natural feel, where the energy and the momentum never fade.

It worked beautifully. Editing is expensive. I saved CBS millions of dollars in editing costs, and I think we maintained a more lively show. That's a win-win situation.

Sometimes we had people fall down coming down the aisle. We left it in. They might fall flat on their faces or go into long stumbles until they eventually tripped over themselves in their excitement. And as many people who fell, we never had one get hurt beyond a bump. Of course, we had pages rushing right out there, helping them get on their feet and up to the stage, and I might make a remark like, "Been drinking again, huh?" or something like that, and we rolled on with the show.

We had situations where models would be pulling on refrigerator doors that didn't open, on cabinets that were stuck, all kinds of gaffes, and we just kept going. The models would be up there tugging on oven doors or on handles or pulling on drawers that wouldn't open, and we made the best of it, all the while getting laughs. I remember one time we had a refrigerator that was stocked with food and sitting on a dolly. They did not shoot the dolly, of course. They just shot the refrigerator and the model whose job it was to open the refrigerator door. When she opened it, the weight of the door was enough to cause the refrigerator to tilt on the dolly and everything in the refrigerator came crashing out on the floor. We left everything in just as it played. I told the audience: "Try to picture this refrigerator without all that stuff lying around it there on the floor. It really is a beautiful refrigerator, you know." I told the announcer, "Go ahead, Johnny, please describe this mess."

A few times on the show we called a common name, "Harry Brown, come on down." Well, it turned out that there were two Harry Browns in the audience, so they both came on down.

Then I'd say, "Now, wait a minute here, is your name Harry Brown?"

"Yes."

And to the other, "Is your name Harry Brown?"

"Yes."

And then I'd turn to Roger Dobkowitz, our producer, or someone who knew which Harry Brown we wanted as the next contestant. "Which one was the one chosen?" I'd ask.

And he'd point out the right Harry Brown.

I'd turn to the other one and say, "Maybe next time," and we'd go on, but it was all on the air.

I remember a show when we called the name of a contestant, and I don't remember if we said "Senior" or "Junior," but they were both in the audience, and they both got up, father and son, and came down. It was the senior that we wanted. I turned to Junior. "What a thing to do, to try to ace out your own father to get on *The Price Is Right*!" I said, "You should be ashamed of yourself. Now, you go back there and sit down." The audience roared with laughter.

Another time, a model accidentally drove a car into a wall. We rolled out this beautiful car with a model at the wheel, smiling into the camera. She smiled and smiled some more as the car rolled—*bam*—into the wall. We just kept going, and I said, "I'm going to give you a chance to win that beautiful car with the dented fender!" and the audience cheered the idea. There were so many moments like that, so many comic episodes and mishaps that we encountered, but we always left them in, and the show was much richer for it.

Of course, the all-time on-air mishap, the one everyone always talks about, was the show with the lady in the tube top.

When her name was called to come on down, she jumped to her feet and began jumping up and down and her breasts popped out of the tube top. She didn't even know it. She got into Contestants' Row, and a lady in the front row told her. She dropped down and pulled her tube top back up. She came on down and "they" came on out on CBS, and no one has ever forgotten it.

I actually didn't see it when it happened. I was waiting behind the doors to be introduced, and when I came out onstage, the audience was roaring with laughter and applauding thunderously. At first I thought it was all for me. I thought: "This audience really loves me!" Then I decided that no audience had ever been that fond of anyone.

I turned to Johnny Olson and asked, "What is going on out here?"

Johnny said, "Bob, this girl has given her all for you."

We left it all in as it played. We put a banner across her chest so you couldn't see anything, but the viewers at home knew full well what happened. That is undoubtedly the most talked about incident in *The Price Is Right* history.

Speaking of Johnny Olson, he was a great announcer and a beloved part of our show. The audiences in the studio and the fans at home loved him. He deserves the credit for the very popular slogan "Come on down." "Come on down" was just three words in the script, but Johnny came up with this delivery, this tone and excitement, and it was magical. It really took off. I am often asked, do I mind or do I get tired of hearing it when people call out to me on the street? The answer is, never. I love it. It means they watch the show. People are always saying "Come on down" to me, and I don't mind at all. I consider it a tribute to the show.

. . .

When people ask why *The Price Is Right* was so successful, my agent always said—as I would expect him to say—that it was all because of the host. But in truth, it was a combination of things. In addition to the spontaneity and the live atmosphere, the basic premise of the show was strong. Everything we did on the show was based on prices, and everyone identifies with prices. You can be a policeman, a doctor, a writer, a cabdriver, but you identify with prices. When we brought out something for the contestants to bid on, the person at home played right along: "Oh, that's a good bid" or "That's not enough" or "That's too much." The viewer at home might be standing at an ironing board or feeding an infant or cleaning the house or doing whatever, but once we get into the price-guessing phase of the show, they're immediately engaged, thinking to themselves, "Well, let's see, that should be about $10" or $200 or whatever the case may be. But whatever they think, they have become involved, and that's what every game show wants. Every show wants viewer involvement, and we had it to the nth degree.

On the subject of prices, I have to confess, I would have been a terrible contestant. I don't know the price of anything. One time a reporter came to do an interview with me, and he brought a grocery bag of items. He said, "OK, you've been asking the questions all these years, now we're going to see how well you know prices."

I did terribly. I didn't know what anything cost.

He said, "No refrigerator for you. In fact, nothing for you, and you better stick to your side of the microphone."

Why should I pay any attention to prices on the show? I couldn't win anyway!

We also had beautiful models—beautiful women who displayed the prizes, demonstrated merchandise, and provided ample grace and beauty to the show. The models were extremely popular with our audience, and along with announcers Johnny Olson, Rod Roddy, and Rich Fields, they became a valuable part of our success. People felt they knew them also. Both our announcers and our models did a fantastic job.

• • •

The Price Is Right was a fast-moving show. We played six games per show, and we constantly developed new ones. We had about eighty games at the time of my retirement. I used to say if you don't like what we're doing right now on the show, wait about four or five minutes, and we'll be doing something completely different. People ask me how I could do that show for so long, and I say because it was always something different every day. Different contestants, different games, different prizes, different audiences—they all had their own unique attraction. Every show was different because you never knew what was going to happen. We played Plinko and some other games once a week. We played some games every other week, and there were others we played less frequently. Our format was so flexible that I could spend extra time with a contestant who was particularly entertaining or funny. If we were having fun and getting laughs, I'd stay with that contestant and make up the time somewhere else in the show.

Someone once said about me that I make my living making other people funny. I think that sums it up. I helped them be funny. I never try to get a laugh at their expense. As a matter of fact, I played straight man for the contestant. I deliberately set them up for a laugh. I think I was able to establish rapport with guests quickly and got them to open up and reveal themselves a bit because they felt they knew me already. I never played any other part on television. I was never a doctor or a detective. I was always Bob Barker: what you saw was what you got. When people would see me on the street or in a restaurant, I was the same guy. People always felt they knew me because they may have watched me for years on *Truth* or *Price,* and I was always just Bob Barker. Also, I had my wife on my shows occasionally. I talked about my pets, and I had them on my shows over the years, too.

After a while, you have established a bond with your audience. I never wanted a contestant to leave with his or her feelings hurt. I wanted them to enjoy every moment of the show, and I wanted them to look back on it as a fond memory in their life. I tried to treat them just as if they were guests in my home. I never tried to put them down. I know there are comedians who do and make a huge success of it, but that's not my style. I tried to have fun with the contestants, and I kidded them, but I hope in a loving way. And we got letters, plenty of them, from people who said being on the show was one of the highlights of their life, one of the best things that ever happened to them. It was always rewarding and encouraging to receive those kinds of letters. I can't take all the credit because our staff did a great job handling people.

• • •

The show had a wide appeal from the beginning, a complete cross section of the country. And I have to say, in all the years

I did *Price,* our audiences and contestants always displayed good manners. They were excited and they could be zany and unpredictable, but our guests always stayed within the boundaries of good taste. We didn't have to bleep out profanities like some shows had to do. I think in general all of our guests knew they were on a family show and acted accordingly. I wanted *Price* to appeal to people of all ages and colors and nationalities. I wanted it to be a show that you could sit down with your mother and watch and not be embarrassed by anything we said or did. And you could.

Our show was different from the others in a lot of ways. Not only did we leave all the unscripted moments in and have packed houses for the tapings of the show, we had contestants that you did not see on other shows. We had ninety-year-olds. I had a winner, a showcase winner, who was ninety-five years old. You never see a ninety-five-year-old on other shows. The fellow was great. I had many people in their seventies and eighties. We had tall, short, fat, thin, old, young, black, white, and brown. We wanted a diverse group. Our country is becoming more and more a melting pot, and we wanted *Price* to reflect that. I believe that is one reason why the show was so successful from the start and for so many years. We had contestants on *Price* who would not get on any other show, and they were wonderful contestants.

I liked working with elderly people, even when I was very young. I always had great fun with them. They say things that are *priceless,* if you'll excuse the expression. One day, I had this older lady come down in Contestants' Row, and she said, "I dreamed about you last night."

I said, "Really? What did you dream? What were we doing in your dream?"

She said, "You were chasing me around the hayloft." You couldn't write things like that.

• • •

During those early years of *The Price Is Right,* we established an enjoyable but professional style and an atmosphere of enthusiasm and fun that would become a trademark of the show for many years. That enthusiasm and joy cannot be faked and it built momentum for the show the longer it ran, but it was all begun in those early successful years. We established loyalty. Later on we would have three generations of family members in the audience who had been watching the show for decades. "Loyal friend and true" became a popular slogan for the show. Somewhere along the line, I had said that to someone on the show and the catchphrase just took off. I received boxes of letters from viewers and audience members who said they were "loyal friends and true," and we had people in the audience with that slogan printed on their T-shirts. It became another symbol of the family atmosphere that surrounded the show.

Most other shows sought out twenty- to forty-year-old contestants who were physically attractive. I think they were missing some great contestants by not broadening their scope to have all types on the air. We had a lot of twenty- to forty-year-olds, too, and plenty of people who were physically attractive, but I insisted on a cross section. I wanted elderly people, I wanted eighteen-year-olds, and we got them.

We had a lot of kids who had just turned eighteen on the

day of the show they attended. You had to be eighteen to be in the audience, and they came to the show on their birthdays to celebrate. Winning a car on *The Price Is Right* made it one memorable birthday. After I retired, I got letters from people who said they wished I had stayed on a little longer because they were just about to turn eighteen, and they had been looking forward to coming on the show for years. That kind of loyalty means a lot to me.

· · ·

People frequently ask me what sort of folks make the best contestants for *The Price Is Right,* and by and large I have to say women make better contestants than men. I have had great contestants of all kinds, and many men have been hilarious, but it seems there are more good female contestants than there are good male ones. It seems that men have more trouble putting their inhibitions aside and just going for it, but when men do, they make great contestants.

Really beautiful women are seldom good contestants. They may be all right, but sometimes I think maybe their beauty has been so prominent that they haven't had to be amusing or interesting vocally. But when you do get a beautiful woman who is funny, too, then you have a winner—a superior contestant. For the most part, I like contestants thirty to fifty years old rather than really young. Perhaps the young ones have not seen enough of life, but often they are a little wary of a situation like being on television. But take a woman of thirty-five or forty, on the other hand, she's lived long enough to know that she's going to survive this, and let's just have some fun.

We also have had handicapped contestants on *The Price Is*

Right. If a person in a wheelchair was called to come on down, a page was prepared to roll them down to Contestants' Row, and then if they won, I'd say, "You win. Come on up here on-stage." Then the page would start wheeling him or her toward the stage. At this point, we would stop tape. In a matter of only a few minutes, the contestant would be prepared to roll onstage. We would start tape and I would say, "Here comes Harry or Margaret to play our next game." If someone had potential as a contestant, being handicapped did not prevent them from being on *The Price Is Right.*

When people came to *Price,* they wanted to participate. They wanted to be contestants. One day there was a lady in the audience who was very pregnant. During a commercial, she gave every indication that she was about to deliver her baby. I asked the pages to help her out, and she said, "I don't want to go. You might call my name." I said, "Madam, we're not going to call any names until you're on your way to the hospital." Fortunately, they got her to the hospital in time for the big event, but she represented people's desire to be on *Price* better than anyone else I ever met.

The Price Is Right was so popular that after three years, Bud Grant, the network head of programming, decided he wanted to make the show an hour instead of half an hour. This was revolutionary. Nobody had been successful with an hour-long game show. It was a bold and audacious idea. He went to Mark Goodson and said, "Do you think you can do this for an hour?"

Mark assured Bud that we could do it. We began playing six games instead of three, and it was then that we added what was to become the famous Big Wheel to the show.

Our format became three games, the wheel, three more games, the second wheel, and the showcase at the end of the show. Not only were we the first game show to succeed as an hour-long show, but our show thrived. In fact, *Price* was even better in the hour-long format than it had been as a half-hour show—because it gave me more time to have fun with the contestants and the audience. Following on the heels of our success, other game shows tried the hour-long format, but all of them struck out.

We had a solid structure and format in place, seasoned people involved in the production of the show, and audience popularity that was unprecedented. We knew we were onto something, but we had no idea that it would last as long as it did. That surprised all of us—but it was a wonderful surprise.

I eventually became involved in the production of the show as well. Frank Wayne was executive producer for eighteen years before I took over. Frank was ill for most of a year, and during that year, Roger Dobkowitz and Phil Rossi, our producers, came to ask me for advice in making decisions. After Frank died, I told Mark Goodson that things were going very well and that I would like to become executive producer and continue as we were. Mark said, "Bob, let's do it," and do it we did, for thirty-five years.

• • •

As I look back now on that incredible thirty-five-year run, I have many happy memories. I loved the whole *The Price Is Right* experience. If there is a theme through this book and my life, it always comes back down to the people, the audiences and contestants. Yes, we had great prizes, and people love to win prizes. We gave away cars and boats and kitchens and living rooms and exotic trips to faraway places. Yes, we had good announcers and support staff, and we had beautiful women displaying the prizes. But everything always came down to the spontaneous energy and entertainment provided by the audience and the contestants. I always said that at *Price* we don't solve the problems of the world, we try to help you forget your problems for an hour. And we succeeded.

To me, the real joy of the show was to watch people reveal themselves and to watch the excitement and humor unfold. It was always fresh because it was always about the interaction with everyday people and the hilarious and heartfelt moments that would occur. That humanity, that humor that everyone has somewhere inside, that is what people were bringing to our show and that is what our show was bringing into living rooms around the country. It was fun to give prizes to people, of course, but the real joy, the real reward of the show, was always the contestants themselves and their personalities, dramas, and stories. You never knew what you were going to find. It was always like mining for gold. I searched for that nugget, that person with whom I could enjoy a really good time. Over the course of thirty-five years with *The Price Is Right,* I was fortunate enough to be in the middle of all that humor, warmth, excitement, and laughter. I found plenty of nuggets, and if you add them all up, I might even go as far as to say, I hit the mother lode.

Contestants and
Celebrities I've Met

While I always loved the contestants on *The Price Is Right,* I have to say that I took my fair share of physical punishment from them over the years. I've been stepped on, kicked, pinched, squeezed, bear-hugged, and manhandled by all kinds of excited contestants and prizewinners. There were plenty of kisses to be sure, but I also remember many black-and-blue moments. There is no way to prepare or to defend yourself from contestants gone wild.

• • •

I remember the painful time I broke a couple of toes. I was limping all over the set of *Price,* and the staff all thought it was funny—everybody thinks broken toes are funny, except people who have broken their toes. When it happened, I was walking barefoot at my house, and I hooked my little toe on a piece of furniture, really banged it hard, and broke the toe. I went to the doctor, but there isn't much the medical profession can do for a broken toe, so he just taped it up.

A few weeks later, when it was finally healing, I was at home, adjusting the clock in the breakfast room. The clock fell off the wall and broke another toe on the same foot with the first broken toe. I couldn't believe it. I called the doctor, and I said, "I've just broken another toe."

He kept telling me that I couldn't have broken another toe. He said, "How sure are you that it is broken?"

I said, "It's pointing in a direction at a right angle to my foot. It's broken. There's no doubt about it."

He told me to go over to the hospital emergency room, and they just did what he did the last time. They put it back in place, taped it up, and sent me on my way.

I got back to the studio to do *The Price Is Right* with one just-healed broken toe and one newly broken toe. One of the first contestants was a woman who looked like trouble as she came up the stairs to the stage. I mean, she was excited beyond reason. She was coming up those stairs like a charging animal. I'm thinking to myself, "How much pain can I stand?" The contestants always stood on my right, and I said to each one, especially this lady: "Please be careful. I have not one, but two broken toes on my right foot."

"Oh, I wouldn't hurt you, Bob," she said. "I would never hurt you."

She won a car, and then she went crazy, jumping all over the stage, and, of course, she stomped on my toe. Pain. Instant agony. But Indians can stand a lot of pain, and I am part Sioux.

. . .

One time I had a woman who was about five feet, four inches tall. She lost control after winning, got underneath my chin, and kept jumping up and down. I endured several teeth-jarring uppercuts to my chin—*bam, bam, bam*—before I broke free. That was one of the most painful experiences I remember. Another woman threw her arms around me, then jumped up and down, and hit me above the eye with her head. She really did a number on my eye. If it had been a fight, the referee would have stopped it for head butting. One woman paused on her way up to the stage, got into a crouch, and then rammed me. I mean she really rammed me, right in the solar plexus, with her head. No explanation. Others would stand beside me and pinch my arm, time after time, saying, "I'm so nervous, I'm so nervous." Just standing in the line of fire, I received plenty of welts and bruises, believe me.

Samoan women seemed to be particularly hard on me. It actually became a running joke on the show, and I got lots of facetious mail about how the Samoan women loved me, but I'll tell you how it all started. We had a lady from Samoa on *Price* as a contestant, and she got so excited when she won a car that she picked me up. I mean, she really hoisted me just like I was a little boy. She wasn't tall, but she was strong and sturdy. She gave me such a squeeze that I could hardly breathe, but I smiled bravely through my pain.

About a year later, another woman from Samoa was a contestant on the show, and sure enough, she won a car. Immediately, this woman picked me up and threw me around like a little boy at a picnic. The audience loved it, of course, and I got kidded a lot, and I received tons of mail about how Samoan women really went for me.

Then, about another year later, yet another Samoan woman contestant came down to Contestants' Row to play for a chance to come on up on the *Price* stage. I was a little leery of the Samoan enthusiasm by now. I stopped and said, "I've been having a problem with Samoan women picking me up and throwing me all over the stage. I want you to swear that if you get up here on this stage and win something, you are not going to pick me up."

She said, "I swear I will not." So lo and behold, she won her way up onstage, she won a car, and then she picked me up higher than either of the other women had and tossed me around.

I said, "I can never go to Samoa. My feet would never touch the sand!"

I did have a few of my own knockouts, however. I mentioned the reunion show we did on *Truth or Consequences* with the Italian woman and her American sister who fainted twice. I had a few women faint on *The Price Is Right* as well. I remember just stepping over one of them and saying, "Get me another contestant, please." I'm kidding. I wouldn't do a thing like that.

I always liked having fun with the contestants on *Price*. I never put them down, but I joked around with them and tried to have fun. When we introduced the wheel to the show, people were nervous about spinning it. Everyone who was familiar with the show had their own theories about spinning the wheel. But they were also nervous because they were on television and they had a chance at all of the prizes and the money, and the audience was cheering and applauding. It can be a little disorienting for contestants—so it was not so surprising that people would spin the wheel—and then they would fall down. They might fall backward, forward, whatever. There was one lady who wouldn't let go of the wheel. She pulled down on the wheel and held on. She shot under the wheel on her stomach, across the hall, and ended up on *The Young and the Restless*. They thought she was an extra and paid her scale. At times when I have told that story, people have asked me, "Did that really happen?" and I had to confess, no, it was just another hallucination.

. . .

As *Price* became more and more popular with many categories of viewers, one of our biggest fan bases was the college crowd. Eventually we had groups of college kids in the studio audience for practically every taping, sometimes three or four of them. It was one of those things that gained momentum, and pretty soon the show was a cult favorite of campuses around the country. Kids came out on spring break from all over. Instead of going to Miami or Palm Springs, they came out to see *The Price Is Right*.

The college student interest started years ago, when a group or two showed up, and I thought, "This is good," so I introduced them. I asked them what school they were from and what fraternity or dorm. I told them thanks for making the trip and that we were glad to have them in our audience, and it caught on. Kids said that they scheduled their classes around *The Price Is Right,* and they watched the show on their dorm television or in recreation rooms with big crowds.

The college students were wonderful audience members and excellent contestants. They brought so much energy to the show. Many of them had been watching the show since they were very young. They knew the games, they asked great questions, and they loved the show. The University of California at Santa Barbara undoubtedly had more kids at our show over the years than any other group. They came down to see us so often I joked with them that there were kids at UCSB who were majoring in *The Price Is Right.* All of the college students knew the show well, and they knew me. They truly warmed my heart.

Sometimes I asked the college students what they were studying, and they might say something like communications.

I'd ask, "What do you want to do?"

And some of them said, "I want to do what you do. I'd like to be an emcee."

"Oh, really," I'd say. "Well, here's a microphone." I asked them to describe for everyone what we're doing, and then I'd let them take the mike. Some of them were remarkably good. Others should change their major.

• • •

On *The Price Is Right,* you had to be eighteen years old to be in the audience, but on *Truth or Consequences,* we had children on the show. Little kids can be marvelous contestants. Art Linkletter had a lot of success working with children. He even wrote a book called *Kids Say the Darndest Things,* and they do. If he will talk, a child is going to get laughs. If a little girl or little boy will talk in a natural way with you and you can't get laughs with him or her, you're in the wrong business.

I frequently had three or four children on *Truth*. If you say to the first kid, "What do you like best of all to eat?" and he says, "I don't know," get away from him. He is going to answer "I don't know" to almost anything you ask, and he can ruin all the other kids. If they find out they can cop out by saying "I don't know," they will do it. If you ask him, "Who controls the money in your family, your mother or your father?" and he says, "My mother does," then you go on with him, you have a place to go. If he says, "I don't know," go on to the next kid until you find one who talks.

Kids can surprise you. One time I selected a young mother and her five-year-old son from the audience. Backstage, they were separated long enough for the mother to come onstage, where I explained that I was going to give her a chance to win some money. How much would depend upon her son. I told her that I was going to ask her son how much she had paid for various items of his clothing, and we would give her whatever he said. I gleefully told our audience that our writers, who had sons, had predicted that she would be lucky to win a dollar and thirty-five cents. Then I asked to have our five-year-old guest join us. Out he bounded. I had chosen him from the audience because of his confident, cheerful, outgoing personality—and he didn't disappoint me. He was all smiles, waving to the audience and admiring himself on the monitor.

I knelt down beside him and managed to get his attention. I told him I had some questions to ask him.

"OK," he answered.

"How much did your mother pay for that jacket you're wearing?" I asked.

"One thousand dollars," he shouted.

The audience exploded into laughter. And they didn't stop. It was one of our biggest laughs ever.

His mother picked up her little hero and smothered him with kisses and the audience continued to laugh.

When sanity was finally restored sufficiently for me to be heard, I said, "I have no more questions."

. . .

People often ask me how contestants have changed over the years. They have changed tremendously in appearance. By that, I mean years ago, most of the people in an audience would be reasonably well dressed. They were going to a television show, and they wanted to look nice. I'm thinking now mainly of *Truth or Consequences*. But even on *Price*, I had contestants wearing a suit or a sports coat. I had many well-dressed ladies and gentlemen in nice sweaters or shirts. Later on, I still had some well-dressed people, but I also began to see casually dressed people. I'd have people in shorts and a T-shirt or sandals and no socks. There were people in jeans and tank tops.

Then, of course, we had the long hair during the hippie period. There were times I would point over to someone in the audience and say, "What about this girl?"

And a man would stand up, with his long hair, and say, "What do you mean, *girl*?"

And, of course, in the last few years of *Price*, I had contestants with pierced noses and ears, even pierced tongues. When

I first started on *T or C,* there probably wasn't a pierced tongue in the entire country.

So audiences and contestants definitely changed in that respect, but I don't find that they have changed a great deal so far as having an interesting or amusing conversation with them. I worked with audiences in the 1950s on *T or C,* and I worked with them in 2007 on *Price,* and I was able to create a fun atmosphere in the same way I did all those decades before. We always had a cross section of all kinds of people on the show, so our appeal was wholesome but widespread. Our audiences and contestants reflected that throughout the years. I think it's a tribute to people and their basic good taste.

. . .

Price was always the more consistent show. We had the games in place, the basic structure was constant, and the audience knew what to expect. We didn't get stagnant, though. We were always fine-tuning, adding new and different games to the mix. But *Truth,* by its very nature, was more of a freewheeling, unpredictable show, and things could go wrong more often. For example, one year we had a national contest involving college football. In those days, the big year-end games were the Rose Bowl, Cotton Bowl, Sugar Bowl, and Orange Bowl. The contest was to pick the winners and the scores of those four games. The person who came nearest to the right winners and scores would win $10,000. This was a lot of money in those days, and we were live.

People sent in their predictions, and we went through all the entries to find the winner after the games. The day arrived when it was time to pay off, and our producer was ill, so Bill

Burch, who was the head writer, had the job of tallying the final entries and picking the winner. Don't ask me how it all happened—it was so many years ago—but he had only a short time to name the winner from the final entries. He came in and gave me the name of the winner. I called the winner at home and congratulated him or her and said, "Your $10,000 check will be on the way." It was a big prize and a big deal, and everybody in the audience was cheering and celebrating when I spoke with the winner on the phone. Then I came off the stage, and Burch was sitting there with his head in his hands, and I said, "What's the matter?"

"I gave you the wrong name," he admitted. He got mixed up trying to figure it out at the last moment and gave me the wrong name.

Now we had a staff meeting. What were we going to do?

Someone suggested, "Why don't you, Bob, call the person we gave it to by mistake and tell him you're sorry there was a mistake made and he won't get $10,000, but we'll send him a refrigerator."

"Bob's not going to do that," I said. "Bob gives people prizes. Bob doesn't take prizes back."

But Ralph Edwards saved the day in his own way. He said, "We'll give the mistake winner $10,000, and we'll give the real winner $10,000."

So Bill's error cost Ralph $10,000. That was just an example of what kinds of things could happen on *T or C*, and, it is also a fine example of Ralph Edwards' good judgment and integrity.

• • •

We always had great prizes on our shows. When we first started on *Truth or Consequences*, we gave away cars occasionally. In those days, a brand-new car was a really big deal. Later on, on *Price,* we would give away whole living-room sets, dining-room sets, incredible vacations, and state-of-the-art appliances, and offered at least two cars on every show. Our ratings were so good that we were coveted by advertisers and prize donors were lining up to place prizes on our show.

On the subject of cars, we eventually made a decision on *Price* to give away only American-manufactured cars on the show. Roger Dobkowitz, the producer of the show, and I were sitting in my dressing room in the early 1980s talking about all sorts of things, and we got to talking about how the American automobile manufacturers were having a tough time. The foreign cars were doing more and more business in the states, so we decided as a gesture to help out the U.S. manufacturers and to support our automobile industry and economy, we would start giving away only American cars. I called Mark Goodson and suggested the change. He liked the idea, and we made the change right away.

Some years later, after Mark Goodson died, there was an executive at *Price* who thought it would be a good idea to start giving away foreign cars as well on the show.

"You could have more of a variety of cars to give away, and they'd be easier to get," he said.

"No, I don't think it is a good idea," I replied. I preferred to stay with what we had been doing.

A little time passed, and he continued to push for the idea. I think he sent me literature and explained that some of the foreign cars were being built in the United States. After he called me a few more times, I continued to stand firm and said, "No, let's stick with what we're doing."

Finally, Roger Dobkowitz came in one day and said he'd been getting calls from the executive suggesting that we start giving away foreign cars.

Then I had an idea. I picked up the phone and called the West Coast branch of the United Automobile Workers, the UAW, and got the top man. Believe it or not, his name was Bruce Lee. I thought, "This is perfect—if I need help, Bruce Lee is the man I want to get."

I said, "We're giving away American-made cars on *Price*, and we are getting pressure to add foreign-made automobiles." I explained the situation to him, and I gave him the executive's name. I asked him if he would give the gentleman a call and let him know that he strongly supported our idea of featuring only American-made cars on *Price*. Mr. Lee said he'd be happy to talk to him, and he would let me know how the conversation went.

Within an hour Mr. Lee called me back and said, "I had a long talk with this fellow, and I don't think he's going to be bothering you anymore. But if he does, you call me again."

I never heard from that executive again. And *Price* is still giving away American cars.

* * *

I could not begin to list all of the celebrities that we had on shows I've hosted, especially *Truth or Consequences*, but we definitely had many legendary entertainers and superstars. Sometimes the celebrities made brief guest appearances or performed, and sometimes they were participants in games and pranks. Certainly, celebrities were always wildly popular with the audience, and it was a privilege and a pleasure to meet so many of Hollywood's giants, as well as sports heroes, record holders, and various other high achievers in assorted fields. Since we were always in the business of getting laughs, we had more than our share of comedians on *Truth or Consequences*. Not surprisingly, they were consistently funny and quick on their feet.

I'm thinking of people like Bob Hope. He was a class act, a marvelous man. We had him on the show. In fact, at one time I had the same agent as Bob Hope. His name was Jimmy Saphier, and he was a well-known, well-respected Hollywood figure. I figured that if he was good enough for Bob Hope, he was good enough for me. And he was. He's the one who signed me for the syndicated *Truth or Consequences*. That was a very profitable deal for all of us.

We had Rowan and Martin on several times when they were first starting out. They were hilarious. They went out and performed in clubs all over the United States, and they let us know when they came back into town because they loved the national television exposure. We put together consequences in which they could be featured and had them on frequently.

One time Dan Rowan played a surgeon. We had an operating-room set, and Dick Martin was his assistant, his nurse, and you can imagine how he assisted. He dropped the scalpel, then picked it up and wiped it on his coat, then gave it to Dan Rowan. The contestant was the patient. Rowan examined him, and he said, "Well, you have . . ." and he made up a long medical term that no one could pronounce. Then

Rowan asked, "Have you ever had it before?" and of course he thought the guy was going to say no. The guy said yes!

At that point, you might think the whole joke was blown, but there was a pregnant pause, and then Martin says, "Well, you've got it again." We had a lot of fun with them. They went on to be very successful, but we had them on first.

We had Joan Rivers on a lot. She was doing clubs in those days, and she was great. She was very funny, and everybody loved her. We had Tony Bennett on the show early in his career. In fact, I used to say we had Tony Bennett on *Truth* before he'd even been to San Francisco. We had Wayne Newton on when he was just starting. He was just a boy, and he was still working with his brothers—they were all musicians.

When he was doing *T or C* on radio, Ralph Edwards came up with the idea to get a town named after the show, and after several cities expressed interest, he settled on a town in New Mexico that had been called Hot Springs. It became Truth or Consequences, New Mexico, and we went down every year for a fiesta. We took lots of Hollywood celebrities because the people down there loved it. We took Wayne Newton down there one year. Nobody knew him in those days, but he was a hit in the fiesta show. He could play any and every instrument you put in his hands. He was a pro then and has been a pro ever since. We took Jayne Mansfield to the fiesta one year. She was lovely. Her husband, Mickey Hargitay, came down as well. He was a great-looking guy, a bodybuilder, and they made a beautiful couple. What impressed me most about Jayne Mansfield was that she had her daughter Mariska with her, and she was such an attentive, loving mother. She may have spent a lot of time being a glamour girl, but she was a great mother, too.

I remember we had Jack Palance on *Truth* in 1953. It wasn't long after he had been a big hit and had been nominated for a Best Supporting Actor Oscar as Jack Wilson, the villain in the movie *Shane*. He was such a great heavy, such a great villain. After the show, Ed Bailey and I went to the Brown Derby and had a drink with him. He was soft-spoken and very gentle. Years later, I remember watching him on television at the Academy Awards as he astounded everyone by doing one-armed pushups. I sat there and said, "Go, Jack, go." We had Bobby Darin on the show in 1958, right after the release of "Splish Splash," his first million-selling hit. The kids in the audience went crazy.

Some of the stars had reputations for being difficult, but when they came on our show, they were absolutely charming. We had Robert Mitchum on *Truth* when he was right at the peak of his career. I was warned that he could be a problem, but he was a perfect gentleman. He could not have been nicer or kinder. He was a great-looking guy, of course, and he impressed everyone on the show with his sense of humor.

Wilt Chamberlain was another excellent guest. In addition to his professional basketball stardom, he was a splendid volleyball player, and for a while he coached the old pro team the Conquistadors in San Diego. I remember when I interviewed him, I was talking to his navel. He was so tall, really amazing. I was quite impressed with him. He came across as very bright, very dignified, and he was quite talkative and very outgoing, a great conversationalist.

I never had Cary Grant on the show, but I had his secretary as a guest along with some secretaries of other famous people. She said, "Mr. Grant asked me to compliment you on your clothes." I thought of all the people I'd like to have compliment me on my clothes, Cary Grant is the man. Later I did have the pleasure of meeting him. One of our writers on *Truth*, Milt Larsen, established the Magic Castle, a popular magic club and restaurant in Hollywood. Cary Grant was always interested in magic. I emceed the annual Academy of Magical Arts awards banquet at the Beverly Wilshire hotel for twenty years. I did it every year for Milt, mainly because I'd do it for free. It was supposed to be a nonprofit organization, and they were charging $20 for a bowl of chili. Milt and his brother Bill ran the organization. I used to get a laugh by saying it's a real pleasure for me to be back again this year doing the Academy of Magical Arts awards banquet for the Larsen brothers, Jesse and Frank.

One year I was doing this magic awards show, and Cary Grant was going to be a presenter. He didn't arrive before I had to go onstage, but I did my introduction for him, and there he was. He came on and did his bit as a presenter. After the show, I was out in the foyer with Dorothy Jo and Irene Lyon, wife of Charlie Lyon, the associate producer and announcer for *Truth* for all those years. We called her Shrimp—everyone called her Shrimp. Shrimp was one of Dorothy Jo's best friends. I went looking for Milt to say good night, and when I walked into a room, there was Cary Grant over in a corner surrounded by people and cameras and newspaper reporters.

He looked over the crowd and shouted out to me, "Hey, Bob! Bob!" He came over and started chatting with me and telling me how well he thought I had done as emcee of the magic awards.

The conversation was going so well that I had the nerve to

say, "My wife and a friend are out in the foyer. Could I bring them in to meet you?"

He said, "Bob, we'll go to meet them."

So we went out, and Dorothy Jo was seated on a little love seat with Shrimp next to her. I came up from behind with Cary Grant and said, "Honey, look who's come to say hello."

Dorothy Jo turned around first and said, "Oh, my goodness."

Then Shrimp turned around, looked up at Cary, and said, "It is . . . it really is!"

Cary was utterly charming. He made it an evening to re-member.

A year later, there was this big dinner before the show, a banquet, and I was at a table with some guests in the giant ballroom of the Beverly Wilshire. Cary Grant comes walking in, and, of course, every eye in the house is on him. And what did he do? He walked right over to my table and said hello to me. I stood up and said, "Good evening, Cary," and we talked for a few minutes. He knew that every eye in the ballroom was on him, and I think that he walked to my table and chatted with me for a few minutes to allow me to share the attention. He was a kind and thoughtful gentleman.

• • •

I'll tell you about another very smooth star, who was also great at comedy, and that was Cesar Romero. We had him on as a guest on *Truth or Consequences,* and he loved comedy, espe-cially slapstick. Here was this suave, well-dressed Latin lover type, but he was always up for any and all kinds of gags we did. He came on the show, sat around with all of us and talked before rehearsal, and he really seemed to enjoy himself. He always said, "Oh, that's great, that's great. Let's do it." One time we were going to fake a hot seat with him, an electrically charged hot seat, and we asked whether he could fake it like he really got jolted. And he said, "Just watch me." When he did it, he came flying out of that seat. He could have won an Academy Award. He was a great guest.

Speaking of Latin lovers, Julio Iglesias was another star with whom I had the good fortune of working. One year, when I was hosting the Miss Universe pageant in New York, Julio sang on the pageant, and he and I ended up staying at the same hotel. As it turned out, our suites were side by side, and we both had balconies. I finally met a man who wanted to be tan as much as I did. Every day before we went to rehearsal, we had enough time to get out there and get sun for a while. As the day wore on and the sun moved, we moved closer and closer to the railing. Eventually we were leaning over backwards off these thick balcony railings, talking to each other. We'd lie there hanging over the edge of the balconies, saying, "What do you think of so and so, Julio?" and, "Yes, that's right, Bob." I wonder if he's still as tan as he was then, or if he's had as many skin cancers as I've had. He was such a romantic singer. And he was a really good guy. He was a lot of fun.

· · ·

I've talked about some of the people in the industry who've had a great influence on my career and on my life, people like Ralph Edwards, Mark Goodson, and my agent Sol Leon, but there's another fellow who I worked with for thirty-five plus years, and he's a good friend of mine to this day. That would be Roger Dobkowitz. At the University of San Francisco, Roger wrote the thesis for his master's degree in communications on game shows. He sent it to Mark Goodson, and Mark was so impressed that he hired Roger to work on *Price* as a production assistant. Over the years, Roger worked his way all the way up to become the producer of the show. As an adult, he's never done anything except work on *Price*. He knows *Price* inside and out. He knows every little nuance of every game, and he's the most creative person on the show. He's developed more games than anyone else. Our original executive producer was Frank Wayne. And when Frank Wayne died, I became executive producer. But I would not have been able to be both host and executive producer if I had not had Roger working with me. He's a fine producer and a good friend.

．．．

The Price Is Right set many records—for longevity, for ratings, and for prizes—and I am naturally proud of the show's many accomplishments. Over the years, CBS did many nice things for me. One that made me particularly happy was that in celebration of our 5,000th show, CBS named Studio 33 the Bob Barker Studio. I did thirty-five years of *Price* in that same CBS studio. So many entertainment legends and people I admired worked and performed and produced shows in Studio 33. Danny Kaye did his show there. Jack Benny, Ed Sullivan, and Red Skelton had their shows there. Carol Burnett and Mary Tyler Moore produced their programs at that studio, and Elvis Presley sang on television for the first time there. But CBS still named it the Bob Barker Studio. That means a lot to me. And it's also a tribute to the show. *The Price Is Right* really took on a life of its own. It became more than a television show. It became a piece of Americana.

Dorothy Jo: Wife and Partner

About two years ago I received an honorary doctorate from my alma mater, Drury University in Springfield, Missouri, and I was asked to give the commencement address. Some of Dorothy Jo's relatives and friends were in the audience. I explained to the graduates and their families that I would not be up there receiving an honorary doctorate if Dorothy Jo Gideon had not become Mrs. Bob Barker. She had graduated summa cum laude and had been the valedictorian of her class. She had also been immediately accepted into George Washington University medical school, which is one of the better medical schools in the Midwest. She threw it all away and married me.

. . .

From the age of fifteen, Dorothy Jo was a part of everything in my life. She certainly deserves a lot of credit for any success

I may have had. It was seventy years ago, but I remember it vividly without even closing my eyes: We had our first date on November 17, 1939. Dorothy Jo was also fifteen years old, and we were together from then until she passed away at age fifty-seven in 1981. She was my wife, my partner, my greatest supporter, and she had more to do with my happiness in life than any other person. She was not just encouraging me from the background. She was right there in the trenches with me in the early years—writing, producing, working alongside me in radio, advertising, and broadcasting. She was by my side throughout my career. She used to say I was a lucky man. She was right. And the best luck of all was having her by my side for so many years.

We met at Central High School in Springfield, Missouri. Jim Lowe, who has remained a loyal friend for all these years, is the one who introduced us. He and I were pals, and in those years he lived just a few blocks from Dorothy Jo. They had grown up together and were good friends. He was going to take someone to see an Ella Fitzgerald concert, and he suggested I ask Dorothy Jo to be my date. I had not met her, but I had seen her, and she was exceptionally pretty and popular. I didn't think she would be interested in going out with me, but Jim said that she would. So I asked her to be my date for the Ella Fitzgerald concert, and she said yes. I was surprised and flattered and proud to be seen with her. We were together from that moment forward. And how about going to hear the great Ella Fitzgerald as a way to start a romance?

Dorothy Jo used to say if Bob Barker has anything, it is tenacity, because I did all those shows, pageants, bake-offs, and parades for so many years. But she was tenacious, too. Also bright, loyal, and loving. My brother Kent surprised me once. He was talking with someone else, and he said he thought Dorothy Jo was the smartest woman he had ever known. I didn't realize that he had figured that out. I knew that she was smarter than I was before the Ella Fitzgerald concert was over.

. . .

I remember another concert we attended back in those days at the Shrine Mosque in Springfield. The band was Tommy Dorsey and his swinging crew. There was a big dance floor and bleachers for sitting. Dorothy Jo and I were sitting up in the bleachers listening to the band when Dorsey announced: "I have a young singer singing with the band for the first time tonight. I hope you all enjoy Mr. Frank Sinatra." And out comes Sinatra. He sang a song called "Indian Summer."

Now, I am tone-deaf. I don't know good from bad, so I turned to Dorothy Jo, and I said, "How is he?"

And she said, "He's pretty good." She was right, wasn't she?

Little did I know that in 1980 I would talk about this very evening with Frank Sinatra himself. I was one of the CBS anchors for the famous Pasadena Tournament of Roses Parade for twenty-one years and I always pretaped an interview with the grand marshal of the parade. The pretape was shown as the grand marshal rode by during the live telecast of the parade on New Year's Day.

Frank Sinatra was grand marshal of the Rose Parade in 1980. As usual, we did our pretaped interview, and afterward we sat and chatted for a few minutes. I told Frank that Dorothy Jo and I had the pleasure of being in the audience that evening at the Shrine Mosque in Springfield, Missouri.

"Frank, was that really the first time you sang with the Tommy Dorsey band?" I asked.

Frank said, "Could've been. Could've been."

Frankly, I have a hunch that Tommy Dorsey did the same introduction for Frank in every city on that series of one-nighters across Missouri. For years, folks my age in Joplin, St. Joseph, Kansas City, St. Louis, et cetera, et cetera—into Oklahoma and points west—have probably been telling their grandchildren and anyone else who would listen that they heard Frank Sinatra the very first time he sang with the Tommy Dorsey band. When quizzed, Frank chose to say, "Could've been. Could've been." Very nice of Frank—not to disillusion us, I mean.

. . .

In high school, I played on the Central High School basketball team and Dorothy Jo was a cheerleader. In my junior year (1939–1940), our basketball team went to Lebanon, Missouri, to play in a regional tournament. It was the highlight of my basketball-playing days. Not only was I the high point man for our team during the tournament, but I was the second-highest scorer among all the teams in the tournament. It was very exciting for me. We won the tournament and I received a small gold basketball as a trophy. When I came home, I gave my gold basketball to Dorothy Jo, and she wore it proudly around her neck all through the rest of high school and college. After we were married, she had that gold basketball put on a charm bracelet along with other symbolic aspects of our lives together. She would wear that charm bracelet when we went on trips, on airplanes, and it was a topic of conversation wherever we went. As the bracelet grew, many mementos from our lives were joined to it, but it started with that basketball. The charm bracelet became huge finally. I have it upstairs in my home, and my gold basketball is still on it.

Incidentally, at the turn of the century, that Central High School team I played on my junior year was named the best Central High School team of the first half of the twentieth century. My senior year we didn't fare as well, mainly because Bob Gentry graduated. Bob was our center and a ferocious rebounder. With Bob gone, we didn't have a top-notch rebounder, and you can't score without the ball.

In spite of the team's decline during my senior year, Drury University offered me a basketball scholarship. I have to thank my high school coach, Jim Ewing, a former Drury star, for putting in a good word for me. In any event, I immediately grabbed the scholarship because Dorothy Jo was going to Drury, so that's where I wanted to be.

I stayed in touch with coach Jim Ewing for as long as he lived. When I was hosting *Truth or Consequences,* we had a stunt that required contestants to shoot free throws. I said, "It's easy. Let me show you how my high school coach, Jim Ewing, taught me to shoot free throws."

Well, I shot and I shot and I shot again. I could not make a free throw. The audience thoroughly enjoyed my plight. I finally made a free throw and we moved on with the show. But the next day I got a telegram from coach Ewing that read, "The next time you shoot free throws on television, please don't mention my name."

Another time, when we were still in high school, we were down at Lake Taneycomo, which is now better known as a suburb of Branson. During my high school years, I worked summers as a bellhop at the hotel, and Dorothy Jo was visiting me. We were sitting on the veranda of the hotel at a table, and there was a deck of cards there that someone had left. Dorothy Jo picked up the deck, and as she was thumbing through them, she turned over the ten of spades. She threw it over to me and said, "Keep that, it will bring you luck." I still carry that card with me. I have carried it my entire life, and it certainly has brought me luck. I never got in an airplane cockpit without it. I keep it in my billfold. I have had it in my pocket for every show I have ever done in my life. Dorothy Jo's lucky ten of spades.

• • •

Dorothy Jo and I were together in high school and college, but I left college after two years to become a naval aviation cadet in World War II. As a cadet, you could not get married until you had earned your wings. Dorothy Jo went ahead and finished college at Drury while I was a cadet. It seemed as if everyone in my cadet battalion got married as soon as he got his wings. It was part of the graduation ceremony: get your wings, go home, get married, and report to your next base with your bride.

I came home on leave to Springfield after I got my wings (which took longer than I expected, but I'll tell that story in a later chapter). Dorothy Jo and I had not planned a wedding, but we knew we wanted to get married. We went down to Ozark, Missouri, to get a license because we wanted to surprise everyone in our town. Her father, Oliver Gideon, was the Greene County assessor at that time, with offices in the courthouse where Dorothy Jo and I would have had to go for our marriage license if we had gotten it in Springfield. So off we went to Ozark. Later, we learned that Oliver knew we had purchased a license in Ozark before we got back to Springfield. Friends of Oliver's in Ozark tipped him off. He was happy, but he was not surprised. Dorothy Jo's parents said they would have a nice wedding for us in Springfield, one with our friends and all the trimmings, if we wanted. Or, they said, they would just give us that money.

"Which do you want?" they asked.

And Dorothy Jo and I said in unison, "We want the money."

We got on the train and headed to St. Louis. I had a hotel reservation in that city, and when we arrived, we went through the yellow pages, found a minister, and went to his home to be married. A friend of mine, a pilot named Howard Hessick, lived just outside St. Louis. He had also gotten married. So he and his wife came and stood up with us at our wedding. It was January 12, 1945, and Dorothy Jo wore a red dress. I still have it. She looked great, and both of us were ecstatically happy.

A coincidence of some magnitude regarding that minister occurred five years later. In 1950, Dorothy Jo and I moved out to Hollywood. We had an apartment on Las Palmas, just below Hollywood Boulevard, and we wanted to go to church one Sunday. We walked up to this Methodist church at the corner of Highland and Franklin, and there was the minister who had married us five years earlier. We were amazed. I'm not sure he remembered us; there were so many young couples who had quick and modest weddings during World War II.

• • •

After we were married, I was stationed in DeLand, Florida, and Dorothy Jo loved it there. We both loved the climate and the sunshine. It was just one of our many shared enjoyments. It was in Florida that Dorothy Jo and I began one of our rituals that would last the entire duration of our thirty-seven years of marriage. It was always difficult to find a place to live during World War II, and when we first went to DeLand, we lived at a hotel. We ate in the singularly unromantic hotel dining room or, worse, in a restaurant. Do not ask me how, but as I might have expected, Dorothy Jo quickly found a charming place for us to live—a three-room apartment in a house—and we moved immediately. I was at the base flying all day, and when I returned, Dorothy Jo had cooked her first meal for us as husband and wife and was all prepared to serve. She brought out a candle and turned out the lights before she called me to dinner. We ate our first home-cooked meal together as man and wife, and it was dinner by candlelight. I remember that dinner vividly—and her face in the candlelight.

As wonderful and romantic as it turned out to be, there was a practical reason she had arranged the candlelight. In addition to cooking dinner, she had also baked an apple pie. The pie was delicious, but the oven was an old one, and for some reason it had made parts of the pie look very black and burned. It was not a burned pie, but it looked burned in a few places, and Dorothy Jo had used the candlelight so I would not see the color of the pie. And that's how our candlelight ritual was born. From that day forward, whenever we were at home dining together, we would dine by candlelight. And that prevailed for thirty-seven years. Even if we just had a sandwich and a bottle of beer, we had it by candlelight.

When I got out of the navy, Dorothy Jo and I went back to Springfield so that I could finish my last two years of college.

She promptly got a job teaching biology at Central High School, and almost as promptly she had the reputation of being one of the most, if not *the* most, popular teacher in the school.

Dorothy Jo was just twenty-one when she became a teacher. She was so young and pretty she looked more like a student than a teacher. Sometimes I would go by the high school to pick her up at the end of the day, and as she walked among the students out to the car, I would think how lucky I was to have her as my wife.

After I got enrolled at Drury, I set about getting a job myself. At first I thought I might try to get a job as a flight instructor at the local airport—all naval aviators qualified as flight instructors upon discharge—but I had no real desire to instruct. I had loved flying, but instructing didn't particularly appeal to me. On the other hand, it seemed wasteful not to use the education and experience I had received in the navy.

Then I heard about the manager of a radio station there in Springfield who was described as "crazy about airplanes," and it occurred to me that such a man just might be interested in having a former navy fighter pilot on his payroll. The station manager's name was G. Pearson Ward, and the station was KTTS. Although I had never even been inside a radio station, I thought it might be fun and interesting to work in one.

I promptly made an appointment with Mr. Ward, and I left nothing to chance. I put on my naval officer's uniform, pinned my wings of gold over my heart, and headed for KTTS. For some reason I've always remembered that Mr. Ward was nicely dressed, wearing a gray glen plaid suit, white shirt, and what appeared to be a silk tie, dark blue. He invited me to sit down in a comfortable chair near his desk and said, "So you were a navy fighter pilot?" During my telephone conversation with Mr. Ward when I made my appointment he had established that I had just been discharged from the navy and that I had flown fighters.

"Yes, sir," I replied.

"What did you fly?"

I told him that most of my time was in the FM-2. It was the original F4F Wildcat with a larger tail and more powerful engine. However, as I explained to Mr. Ward, I had checked out in the F4U Corsair, been placed in a fighter pilot pool, and had the war not ended, I would have joined a seagoing squadron flying Corsairs.

Mr. Ward listened so intently to everything I said about airplanes that I got the distinct feeling that if he had been younger, he would have loved to have been at the controls of a Corsair himself during World War II.

After about thirty minutes of talking about dogfighting, dive-bombing, and carrier landings, I had my first job in radio. Mr. Ward did take me into a studio and have me read about one minute of sports copy, but that seemed almost secondary. I went home and told Dorothy Jo that I was going to work at radio station KTTS, and she asked a perfectly sensible question: "What do you know about radio?"

I answered honestly: "Absolutely nothing."

• • •

I started out writing local news for news editor Bill Bowers, a former vaudeville hoofer who had become a really dedicated newsman. Also, I did a five-minute sportscast. It was spon-

Above: My first publicity picture for *Truth or Consequences*. Right: Sign for *The Bob Barker Show*.

Right: A publicity photo of Dorothy Jo taken for the Southern California Edison radio show, around 1952. Below: Ralph Edwards and me with his "Aren't we devils?" pitchfork.

Above: At the
Ambassador Hotel
in 1957, with Ralph
Edwards and Bill
Leyden, host of *It
Could Be You*, another
of Ralph's shows.
Left: One of the
first publicity
shots for *Truth or
Consequences*.

Above: My mother surprises me on *Truth or Consequences*, 1957.
Right: *Truth or Consequences* staff (left to right): Dresser Dahlstead, Charlie Lyon, Ed Bailey, Jerry Payne, me, and Ralph Edwards.

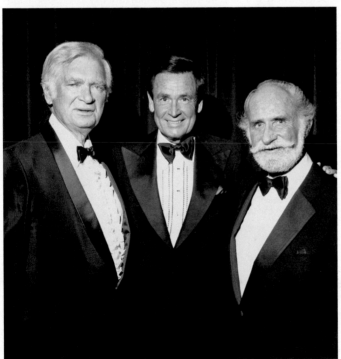

Above, left: Robert
Mitchum and me
with contestants
on *Truth or
Consequences*.
Above, right: With
Gloria Swanson
on *Truth or Conse-
quences*. Left: Buddy
Ebsen, me, and
Keenan Wynn at the
Beverly Wilshire hotel
in 1980.

Above: My brother, Kent Valandra, his wife, Beth, me, and Kent's son Bob at the 5,000th show taping of *The Price Is Right*. Below: Henri Bollinger, me, and Les Moonves celebrating a *Price Is Right* season in my dressing room after the show.

Above: The staff of *The Price Is Right* at the end of the 35th year—my last season. Left: With Cary Grant, 1970s.

Right: With Dick Clark at the Emmys. Below: Being installed as a member of the sheriff's posse in Truth or Consequences, New Mexico. Opposite: Roger Dobkowitz and me on set at the end of the 33rd season of *The Price Is Right*.

Right: Me (on left), Walter Baker, and James (Dolly) Brazeale, during practice for the 1940–41 Central High basketball team in Springfield, Missouri. Below, right: Gene Sparlin and me shortly after the basketball tournament in Lebanon, Missouri; this photo was originally printed in the *Springfield News & Leader*. Below: Dorothy Jo and me during our freshman year at Drury; this photo was originally printed in the *Springfield News & Leader*.

Gene Sparlin guards Robert Barker, who won a first-string berth with his hangup performance in the Lebanon regional tournament.

"YOU'RE lovely and sweet and dance divine. Please, Won't you be my Valentine?" were the sentiments of handsome Bob Barker, Drury Sigma Nu, as he dipped and twirled at the Tri Delta sweetheart dance with best girl Dorothy Jo Gideon.

Left: Dorothy Jo and me just after we married, when we returned from St. Louis. Below: Dorothy Jo, age twenty. She sent me this photo when I was in the navy. Bottom: Working as a disc jockey at KTTS, 1946.

Above, left: Age four in Pampa, Texas. Above, right: Age 5 in Brownsville, Texas. Right: Age twelve with Brownie on the reservation.

To our dear friend Tillie and her delightful family
our best wishes Alice and Ben Reifel ML 1961-62

Above: In Washington, DC, in 1962 with Alice Reifel, my mom, Ben Reifel (the first Sioux Indian elected to the House of Representatives), and Dorothy Jo. Below: With Whitey Herzog, manager of the St. Louis Cardinals.

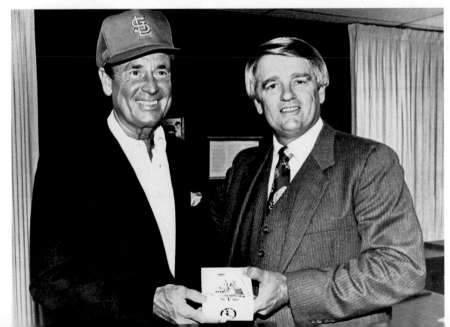

Matilda Tarelton, John Bonde, Ruth Maxwell, taken in Mitchell, S.D., during the Corn Palace Days 1918.

Top: A photo of my mother at the wheel of an automobile from an Arlington, South Dakota, newspaper, 1918.
Above: At age twelve sitting on the bumper of Mother's Chevrolet (in which she taught me to drive) in Mission with Brownie. Right: Playing basketball for the navy, 1944.

Left: In my navy greens, 1945. Below: Me and Dorothy Jo with Suerte, Juan, and Carlos. Following page: With Federico. This is my most popular fan photo of all time.

sored by Hires Root Beer, and I opened it by saying, "Hire's to ya," in a cheery, happy voice, as if I were saying hello to a friend. The sportscast didn't last long. But over a period of a year or so, I did news on the air; I became a staff announcer; I had a disc jockey show; I did anything and everything that I had a chance to do at the station.

As I have admitted, I'm tone-deaf. I was probably the only tone-deaf disc jockey they ever had in Missouri. Oh, probably not! But I faked it. I always had a copy of *Down Beat* magazine at my fingertips and told my listeners who was on drums, who was on the clarinet, who did this riff and who did that riff (by the way, what's a riff?).

I did my first remote broadcast at KTTS. I had all my classes at Drury in the morning so that I could work the afternoon shift as an announcer. One day Mr. Ward called me and told me to stay at Drury after my last class because they were going to lay the cornerstone for the new field house and he wanted me to do a live broadcast of the ceremony. Mr. Ward said he was sending Homer Hubbel, one of our engineers, over with all of the equipment and I should meet Homer at the site of the future field house.

I said, "Yes, sir!" I was delighted. It was to be a live remote broadcast, my first one. Look out, Ed Murrow, here I come!

After my last class, I went down where the cornerstone ceremony was to be held, and there was Homer, all ready to get it on. As promised, Homer had all the equipment in his car. He gave me a hand microphone that had the call letters KTTS across the top and told me that we would go on the air live in about five minutes.

However, the crowd gathering for the ceremony was much larger than anyone had expected, and with about three minutes to go before airtime, I said, "Homer, I can't see a thing."

"Quick, get on top of my car," Homer replied.

I put the hand mike in my coat pocket, and as fast as I could, I clambered up on Homer's car. Homer alerted me: "You have one minute, Bob."

I reached into my coat pocket for the hand mike, and to my horror, I couldn't get it out of my pocket. The call letters KTTS had become entangled in the lining of my coat. Homer cautioned me: "Thirty seconds, Bob." I pulled and hauled on the hand mike to no avail.

Homer began a ten-second countdown: "Ten, nine, eight, seven . . ." The hand mike was still tangled up in my coat pocket. ". . . Six, five, four, three, two . . . You're on!"

And I did the only thing I could. I pulled my coat up to my face and spoke into my coat pocket. "Good afternoon, KTTS listeners. We are live at the cornerstone ceremony for the new field house on Drury College campus. . . ." That's how I described the entire affair, speaking into the pocket of my coat.

When we got back to the station, Mr. Ward complimented Homer on the quality of the sound during the remote. Homer didn't tell Mr. Ward that the sound was "filtered."

* * *

I had taken the job at KTTS to augment my income from the GI Bill while I finished my degree at Drury, but I enjoyed working in radio so much that I thought I would like to stick with it after I finished school.

As I mentioned earlier, I did anything and everything that I got a chance to do at KTTS. But if I wanted to make a living in radio, particularly on a network level, I knew that I should choose one thing and concentrate on becoming as good as I possibly could at it. As usual, I discussed the matter with Dorothy Jo, but we didn't come to a decision. We agreed that I should continue getting experience in various facets of radio and that we would talk more about it.

Eventually, I got an opportunity to host an audience participation show, talking with people out of a studio audience—the type of thing I did for fifty years on television. Dorothy Jo listened to that first show, and when I got home, she said, "That's what you should do. You did that better than you have ever done anything else." She didn't say I was good. She just said I did it better than I had ever done anything else. From that day forward, Dorothy Jo and I worked together with one goal in mind: to get me a national audience participation show.

Before I left KTTS, with Dorothy Jo working right beside me, I had done shows from a studio we had at the station, from a drugstore, a grocery store, a theater, and out on the street. All of these shows required ideas and then more ideas. They also needed writing, research, questions and answers, and staging. Dorothy Jo was right at my side all of the way, doing her share and more. Of course, she was still teaching, too. But she and I worked evenings and weekends—vacations, too.

• • •

In early 1947, I heard very good things about a summer radio course taught at the Pasadena Playhouse in California. Dorothy Jo and I talked it over, and decided that when I graduated from Drury in June 1947, I should go out to California and take the course.

Then, much to our delight, we learned that our friend Jim Lowe, who was graduating from Missouri University at the same time, was going to California to take a course sponsored by NBC. Of course, Jim and I decided to drive out together, and as a result, we shared a piece of American history: we were among the first drinkers to imbibe on what was to become the legendary Las Vegas Strip.

We drove into Las Vegas, and all the lights, all the people, and all the action was in downtown Las Vegas. But Jim and I were curious about comments we had heard concerning a new casino called the Flamingo. Some of the comments were hopeful, even optimistic. Some comments were snide. Jim and I decided to check out the Flamingo for ourselves. We drove clear out of Las Vegas and into the desert. There, surrounded by nothing but more desert, was the Flamingo, a work in progress, and apparently progressing too slowly in the opinion of some of the investors.

We were told that the Flamingo was the idea of Benjamin "Bugsy" Siegel. Mr. Siegel thought that a beautiful casino with top talent to entertain would attract big spenders from Los Angeles. When Jim and I visited the Flamingo in the summer of 1947, only the bar was open. Everywhere else there were cranes and carpenters. Jim and I had our drinks—Rob Roys, as I recall—and split. That summer, while Jim was honing his radio skills at NBC and I was doing the same at the Pasadena Playhouse, Mr. Siegel was shot to death in Beverly Hills. I read that his demise was probably arranged by some of his disgruntled business associates.

They jumped the gun—pun intended. I was in Las Vegas recently, and when I stood in front of the Flamingo, I saw nothing but more hotels for miles in every direction. Mr. Siegel was right on, but he should have chosen business associates who were not so impatient.

I don't know how much his experience at NBC that summer had to do with it, but Jim Lowe ended up as one of the most popular disc jockeys in New York City. In 1953, Jim wrote a megahit song called "Gambler's Guitar." It was recorded by Rusty Draper, a popular vocalist of the time, and stayed on the charts for weeks. In 1957, Rusty Draper was still hot, as Hollywood folks say, so our celebrity booker suggested that we invite Rusty to do a guest appearance on *Truth or Consequences*. It wasn't my idea, but I was all for it. Rusty agreed to do *Truth,* and suggested that a young friend of his join him. His friend was attracting attention for his work as a cowboy on a television Western, *Laramie,* and we readily agreed.

After Rusty and his friend had done their bit on *Truth,* I chatted with them for a few minutes, and I remember thinking, "That young cowboy may do OK in Hollywood." His name was Clint Eastwood.

After my summer radio course, I worked at KTTS for another year, and then, after a stop in Palm Beach, Florida, Dorothy Jo and I headed west. To be more specific, we headed for Hollywood. After all, it was in Hollywood and New York that the national radio shows originated, and it was a national radio show that we were after.

I bought a two-wheel trailer, loaded all of our worldly goods in it, and away we went. Now, I had never driven a car pulling a trailer, and we weren't out of the Palm Beach city limits before I realized that there is more to pulling a trailer than you might think (until you have experienced the thrill of pulling one). We were in a violent windstorm most of the way across Oklahoma, and by virtue of the fact that we survived, my confidence mounted tremendously. By the time we reached Hollywood, I could back that trailer up and even park it—if the parking area was a bit spacious.

Incidentally, when we got to Hollywood, I sold the trailer for more than I had paid for it. It was one of my better investments.

My Years on the Reservation

People often ask me, "When you were little did you always want to be a television host?" Some are surprised to hear that when I was a child, there was no television. It was a different world then, especially for a boy growing up in South Dakota. This was the 1930s in some of the most rural and rugged parts of the country, but it was also spectacular territory in which to spend a boyhood because I developed a love of the outdoors, physical activity, sports, and adventures of all kinds. Growing up in South Dakota nurtured in me a reverence for nature and a love of animals.

As a child, I had no notion of historical context, but as I look back, the challenges that my mother and other South Dakotans faced in those years were extraordinary. The 1930s began with the worst drought and grasshopper plague ever experienced in the state. The drought, accompanied by dust storms, lasted for ten years (except for some relief in 1932 and 1935), and the Great Depression (1929–1939) also caused thousands of South Dakotans to lose their jobs and their land.

• • •

My mother and I moved to Mission, South Dakota, when I was six years old, right after my father died in 1929. I went to school from the second grade through the eighth grade in the Mission, South Dakota, public grammar school, which was only two rooms large. On the subject of my father, I can still remember near the end, when he was sick. He was so ill he was bedridden. He was at home, and he called me into his room. I was called Billy for much of my youth, and I remember he said, "Billy, when you become a man, promise me you will always take care of your mother." In later years, I realized that my father's request indicated that he knew or at least thought there was a possibility that he was terminally ill.

I assured my father that I would always take care of my mother, and many years later, I had the opportunity of caring for her when she was elderly, and eventually ill. She lived with me in Hollywood for years when she was older. I kept my word to my father. Though he died when I was very young, I do remember him.

My father liked to box. He had boxed as a younger man, and my mother said he would go to Omaha to watch professional fights. I remember he bought me some boxing gloves, and he would get on his knees and box with me. He was, according to my mother, an incredible cardplayer and a pretty successful gambler at cards. Mother said he was wearing custom-made suits and silk shirts and driving a big car when she married him, but she told him if they were going to be married, he had to concentrate on electricity—he worked on the power lines—from then on. Mother said that between electrical jobs, my father would tease her, saying, "Tilly, maybe I should go find a card game."

My mother and father had a lot of fun. Apparently, he was an adventurous guy. Mother told me that before she married my father, he and a friend rode motorcycles down to Mexico. They met Pancho Villa in a bar. Pancho Villa took them with him and his friends to a bullfight. Mother said that my father was aghast at the blood spectacle. He could not stand to see the cruelty to the animal, and he left the bullfight. Maybe some of my animal protectionist streak is genetic.

My mother also told me that after I was born, she had gone to an astrologer, who told her that this baby was going to make his living talking. My mother immediately thought I might follow in my grandfather's footsteps and become a minister, or she thought I might become an attorney, speaking in court. Television did not exist, and radio was in its infancy. But sure enough, I went on to make my living all my life by talking.

• • •

When Lewis and Clark first explored the area, South Dakota was Indian territory, and as I was growing up, there were still many Native Americans living there. According to the census of 1930, out of a population of 692,849 people, approximately 3 percent of those residents were Native American. In Mission, a farming town on the Rosebud Reservation with a population of only 200, probably one-third of the residents were Native Americans. My father was one-quarter Indian. His mother was one-half Indian. I am one-eighth Sioux. It was not uncommon to have Indian heritage in those days in that region of the country. My stepfather was one-half Indian.

As I mentioned, I was called Billy for much of my childhood. My father's name was Byron John Barker. He did not like Byron or John, so everyone started calling him Bill. When I was born and named Robert William Barker, they called him big Bill and me little Bill. Then I was Billy. I was Billy Barker all through childhood. My mother called me Billy, and all my friends called me Billy. Eventually, I had to change it while I was at school in Mission, South Dakota, probably in the third grade. The school was approximately 75 percent white and 25 percent Native American. The government was always interested and always checking to see whether the Indians were in school or not, and I was part Sioux, so they were interested in my attendance.

Since I always signed everything Billy Barker, there was some confusion at the Office of Indian Affairs, and my mother often received letters asking whether Robert William Barker was going to school. One day my mother said, "You are going to make this easier on me. You are not Billy anymore. You are Bob." I went to school and I told my teacher that from now on I was Bob. And I have been Bob ever since. Curiously, many of my professional colleagues, on both shows, called me Barker. Many of my close friends called me Barker for years. Even my wife and my brother called me Barker.

The funny thing about that incident back in the third grade was that as soon as my classmates heard of my new name, they all wanted to change their names, too.

"I want to be Helen."

"I want to be Ralph."

"I do not like Irene. I want to be Ruth."

"From now on I am Donald."

Everybody wanted to change his or her name. My name change made life easier for my mother, but it was tough on my teacher.

• • •

As I observed earlier, only two hundred people lived in Mission. There was no municipal government, no water system, no sewage disposal, no electricity, and most of the time, no doctor. We called the town the Paris of the Prairie.

There was an Indian boarding school about two miles east of Mission. Our high school basketball team played its games in the boarding-school gymnasium, and it was in that gym where I first saw the Harlem Globetrotters play. Cowboys, Indians, and town folks filled the gym to overflowing that night. They absolutely adored the Globetrotters! Who doesn't?

I played my first organized basketball in the boarding-school gym. I played on the Mission Midgets. We didn't have uniforms, so we wore undershirts—the kind Clark Gable made popular in *It Happened One Night*—and any kind of shorts we could dig up. The other mothers cut out numbers and sewed them on their sons' undershirts. My mother sewed a question mark on mine. She thought that was pretty funny. So did everyone else.

Just down a hill south of Mission was Antelope Crick. That's the way everyone in town pronounced it: "crick," not "creek." And about three miles west of Mission there was a large dam. We used to go down to Antelope Crick and swim as soon as the water was warm enough to get in. South Dakota summers are hot, and we would run down the hill and dive in the crick several times a day—six times in one day was the record.

Of course, we didn't bother with swimsuits. We just tore off the few clothes we had on and dived in. We never wore shirts in the summer. We took our shirts off the minute school was out and didn't put them on again until school started in September. That's why I have paid for so many vacations for Beverly Hills dermatologist Steven Weiss. (I promised Dr. Weiss's mother I would mention his name in my book.)

The only road into Mission from the south crossed the mighty Antelope, so, of course, there was a bridge over the crick and we thought it was great sport to dive from the bridge. Now, there never was a problem with gridlock, or anything resembling gridlock, on this one road into Mission from the south. But there was an occasional automobile, and occasionally it was driven by one of the ladies of the town.

It seems that these ladies resented seeing naked boys flying through the air as they drove over the bridge, and in desperation, they took their problem to the city fathers, one of whom came down to the crick one day and in no uncertain terms told us to cease and desist with the skinny-dipping or they—the city fathers—would see that we had to pick up every tin can in Mission. And there were a lot of tin cans in Mission.

We took the matter very seriously, and in the future we were careful to dive into the crick before a car got to the bridge. When the ladies of the town drove over the bridge, all they saw were happy little faces smiling up at them.

Which brings me to the dam. The dam west of Mission was great for ice-skating. It was a really large dam for such a small town, and in winter we took full advantage of it. We skated and played our version of hockey. One day I was trying to do something a little fancier than any of my friends had ever done on skates. My feet went flying up over my head and the first part of me to hit the ice was my right eye. I was cut; I was bruised; I was swollen—I was a mess. My friends were actually concerned about me, and generally they scoffed at everything. When I went home, I opened the door and my mother screamed. Then she asked, "Have you been in a fight?" I said, "Yes, and I lost to the ice." But I lived to skate another day.

. . .

Those years in the tiny school in Mission, South Dakota, were some of the most educational of my life. It all came together then. Those seven years were the foundation of my education. My mother was an educator. I was in a small schoolhouse with several grades grouped together, whites and Indians. There was no discrimination then as I remember, and I had white friends and Indian friends. We all played sports together and played on teams together. It was a simple life, but it was an environment that fostered and satisfied my love of both sports and reading. There was something about that South Dakota geography—that territory of blue skies, mountains, and rivers, and the rugged terrain—that produced excellent athletes. There were some Indians in that school and in that area who were splendid athletes. We ran. We swam. We played basketball, baseball, and football.

My uncle owned a pool hall in Mission, and that was the center of social activity in the town. I remember that my uncle taught me to play pool, and for a while I was the best seven-year-old pool player in that part of South Dakota. I was pretty small, so I had to get up on a stool or something, I remember. But I was good.

. . .

The harsh winters also offered me plenty of opportunity to read, and I developed a voracious appetite for young adventure books. I read all the Rover Boys books. I read all the Tom Swift books. I read *Tom Sawyer,* and I started to check out *The Hunchback of Notre Dame,* thinking that it was a football story. The kindly librarian straightened me out. I liked books on sports. I enjoyed adventure stories, and I liked to read about military heroes. I never cared for comic books, but I liked sports magazines and Western magazines. There were some great sports pulp magazines.

Another of my favorite series was the Boy Allies books. They were written about two American boys who volunteered for the French army during World War I. My favorite pulp magazine was *G-8 and His Battle Aces.* They were pilots during World War I. G-8—that was his designation because in addition to being a splendid pilot who shot down countless Germans, he was also a spy. Nippy Weston was G-8's wingman, and Bull Martin, an all-American football player, was the other. G-8 was always doing marvelous things with makeup and disguises. He carried makeup with him, and he would get behind enemy lines and transform himself. He would knock some guy out, and then reappear looking identical to him. It was a pulp magazine that came out once a month, and I could not wait to get up to the print shop and see what adventures G-8 and his battle aces had pulled off. Those were such exciting stories.

One time I was playing golf at Bel Air, and I hit a ball out-of-bounds. I said out loud to myself, "Oh, G-8 would have been disappointed with that." My golfing partner shot me a look of disbelief.

"Did you just say G-8? Did you read G-8?" he asked. He, too, had been a boyhood believer, and after that, we talked the whole rest of the round about *G-8 and His Battle Aces.*

• • •

As a boy, I loved baseball. I never wanted or even thought about going into show business when I was little. I have often said all I ever wanted to do was pitch for the St. Louis Cardinals professional baseball team, and the only thing that stopped me was a complete lack of talent.

In 1983, I was in St. Louis to host the Miss Universe pageant at the Kiel Auditorium, and someone in the Cardinals office had read or heard an interview in which I had said that my boyhood ambition had been to pitch for the Cardinals. So he invited me out to the ballpark.

Whitey Herzog was the manager of the Cardinals at that time. He gave me a handsome Cardinals jacket that I still wear and a Cardinals bag that I carried until it was in tatters. When my Cardinals bag finally disintegrated, Sue MacIntyre, coproducer of *Price,* called her mother, who lived in St. Louis, and had a new one rushed to me before I went into a depression. In addition to giving me my Cardinals jacket and bag, during my visit to the ballpark, Cardinals manager Whitey Herzog signed me to a contract with the St. Louis Cardinals baseball team. Under the terms of the contract, I receive a dollar a year from the Cardinals, so long as I do not pitch.

Whitey said that if he sees me even warming up, the contract is null and void.

Naturally, my father's dying young was a tragic blow to me and my mother, but nevertheless, I still look back on my childhood as a wonderful time, and I have many vivid memories of marvelous activities and lasting friendships. My first friend that I can remember, from a very young age, was a little fellow named Jesse Goins. This was actually before we moved to South Dakota. We were still in Springfield, Missouri, and I was younger than six years old. Jesse was a year older than me, and he lived near my grandmother. He was a lot of fun. He was not only bright but extraordinarily talented. He could play the guitar and sing, even at that young age. This was southwest Missouri. Plenty of music around there, and this boy could really play. He was hardly able to hold the guitar, but he was so good that he went on the radio when he was in the third grade. He became a successful country-and-western musician. Very successful with the ladies, too, I guess. Jesse died at an early age, and his mother said, "It was the women who did it. The women just wouldn't let Jesse alone."

Jesse was also the first person, the first of many I might add, who told me I could not sing. I remember he was at my house one time, and he had his guitar. He was singing and playing, and he said, "Sing with me." So I started singing. When we stopped, he looked at me, and he said, "Billy, you don't sing, you talk the words." I suppose that was his way of saying I was way out of tune. He was absolutely right. I could not sing then. And I never could sing.

Another time, after we had moved to South Dakota, my mother and I went to the Episcopal church. My grandfather had been a Methodist minister, but there were only three churches in town for us to choose from—Catholic, Episcopal, and Lutheran. Anyway, I went to Sunday school, and the church decided it was going to have a choir. They had no auditions or anything. They just said, "Go on, Billy, you are in the choir."

I carried the cross into the church and led the choir into the church, and one day the minister, Reverend Barber, said he wanted the choir to stay after church and sing a hymn. So we stayed and he gave us a hymn, and we all sang it. He went by and listened to each little boy who was singing. He was apparently satisfied because he soon let everyone go, but after the others left, the reverend came up to me and said, "Billy, you can stay in the choir. You can still carry the cross. But when the others sing, you just move your lips."

I never sang again. (I used to be a frequent guest on *The Dinah Shore Show* and Dinah tried constantly to get me to sing. No dice.)

• • •

It was not all school and play back then. As I grew older, I did start to work at various jobs. My first job as a boy was pumping water for Shorty O'Connor's café in Mission. There was no water system, and I pumped water out of an artesian well for him. That was my first job ever. I also sold magazines, *Collier's* and *Boys' Life,* and newspapers, the *Minneapolis Tribune* and the *Omaha Bee News.*

But my favorite job as a kid came later, when I was in high school in Springfield, Missouri. About sixty miles south of Springfield, there is a summer resort on Lake Taneycomo called Rockaway Beach. It is in Taney County, Missouri (hence

"Taney Co-MO"—get it?). Charlie White was a teacher at Central High, and he managed Hotel Taneycomo down there at the lake every summer for a man named Merriman. Mr. Merriman was with the Armour Food Company in Chicago. He owned this beautiful hotel, and he had a lovely home on the beach as well. As the manager of the hotel, Charlie would take five boys every summer to go down to Rockaway to work as bellhops. I went down there for three years, after my sophomore, junior, and senior years of high school.

We bellhops lived in a tiny little cabin called the Owl's Roost. The hotel itself had a long beautiful lobby, appropriately rustic. There were cottages all up the hillside. We were paid only $10 a month, but we got room and board and our tips. I made enough there every summer to last me through the next school year. I had some great friends on that job with me. Jim Brown went on to become a successful surgeon. Jim Calloway was another friend. He became a naval aviator and flight instructor. Walter Baker became very successful in the cement business in Memphis.

In addition to being bellhops, for a brief time, Jim Brown and I were involved in another caper. At that time you could not buy liquor on Sundays. People would check into the hotel and want to buy liquor, but since it was Sunday, they were out of luck. Being the enterprising young men that Jim and I were and always looking to provide service to the guests, we decided that we would buy the liquor and then resell it to the guests at a very profitable margin. This worked splendidly for about three weeks. We had said it was capitalism at its best. Then Charlie White told us one day that the owner of the liquor store wanted to see us. We went over there, and the gentleman explained to us that we could call it whatever we wanted, but, he said, we were bootlegging, and if we did not stop, we were going to be incarcerated. He was polite, but he was very effective. Jim and I immediately abandoned that business endeavor.

All of us bellhops had a grand time working at Rockaway Beach. Dorothy Jo came down to visit me sometimes. Sometimes I hitchhiked home to see Dorothy Jo, or I would get a ride with the mail truck. Often she and I would go hear a big band play at the Shrine Mosque—among them Glenn Miller and Artie Shaw. At the end of the weekend, she drove me out to the highway, and I hitchhiked back to the hotel.

The job of bellhop at Rockaway Beach was a coveted assignment that every boy at Central High School would have liked to have had. We had as much fun, if not more, than the guests. There was a dock and a pier with lots of room to lie in the sun. We had the best tans on the beach.

Johnny Kidd and His Louisianans played every night at the dance pavilion, and the bellhops got in free. Dorothy Jo and I danced away many a night there. She was a great dancer. I didn't dance very well . . . but I danced better than I sang.

I got a lot of mileage out of telling my friends about checking singer/actor Tony Martin into Hotel Taneycomo, and like all bellhops, I remember his generous tip.

I look back at bellhopping at Hotel Taneycomo on Rockaway Beach with the fondest of memories.

• • •

I am eternally grateful to my mother for seeing to it that I had an active and educationally rich childhood. She was devoted to education and to me, and she made sure I got the maximum benefits out of my schooling experience in the South Dakota school system. Both of my parents contributed significantly to my love of nature, my love of sports, and my love of animals. They were dynamic, physically active people who loved to travel, loved to read, and were always kind to other people. They taught me to believe in myself and to treat people with dignity and respect. When I look back on my childhood and my youth, I am immediately reminded that it was all made possible by the love and care provided to me by my mother and father, for the few years he had with us.

Tilly–What a Mom!

I have often said that the three most influential people in my life were Dorothy Jo, Ralph Edwards, and my mother, Matilda, or Tilly, as she was called. I have written about Dorothy Jo and some of the wonderful years we had together, and of course, Ralph Edwards gave me my first opportunity on national television and became a dear friend. But first there was my mother. She was the one who raised me single-handedly from a young age after my father died. She was an extraordinary woman, and she taught me, loved me, encouraged me, and instilled in me values and principles that have carried me and benefited me throughout my life and career. As I have said, I have lived a blessed life—and without a doubt, one of the most profound blessings of my life is the love and upbringing I received from my mother.

. . .

My mother, Matilda Kent Tarleton, was born on October 18, 1898, in Eminence, New York, the daughter of a Methodist minister. He had come over from Ireland and had met my grandmother in Eminence, New York, where he had a church and preached regularly. They had five daughters and a son. One of the daughters had a respiratory problem, and the doctors suggested that they move to a drier climate. They chose South Dakota. The winters are very cold there, but South Dakota is dry. He preached in Miller, South Dakota; Arlington, South Dakota; and ended up in Hot Springs, South Dakota—which is out in the Black Hills, an absolutely beautiful part of the state.

Once I asked my mother why my grandfather moved from church to church as he had. She laughingly replied, "Maybe he did it so that he could use his best sermons more than once." I don't know whether she was kidding or not.

Mother told me about a young male goat that her father brought home one day. She described the goat as a real character. Immediately upon arrival, the goat considered himself a full-fledged member of the family, and that's the way everyone treated him.

When the children ran and played outside, the goat joined in and enjoyed every moment of it. Although he continually tried to come into the house, apparently my grandmother drew the line at that. However, the goat did find a way to check up on what was going on in the house. He learned to get up on the chicken coop and watch the family through a large living-room window.

One day my grandmother made grape jam and threw the grape skins out into the trash, where the skins fermented. This curious goat found the fermented grape skins, and of course, he ate them. A bit later, someone looked out a window, and said, "Quick, come look at this goat."

My mother said the goat was prancing around on its hind legs, waving its front hooves in the air. She said he looked every bit as if he were dancing. My grandfather must have had some idea of what was wrong with the goat. He went straight to the trash and confirmed that the fermented grape skins were missing. My grandfather turned, came back into the house, and said, "That goat is drunk!"

When my mother graduated from high school in Arlington, South Dakota, where she was valedictorian of her class, she left home permanently. She went to college in Mitchell, South Dakota, at Dakota Wesleyan University. Her decision to leave home and seek educational achievements was typical of my mother. She was very independent, and she always put a high value on education of all kinds. While she was in college, she worked in a grocery store, paying for her room and board, and she always garnered good grades. Mother was the oldest of the six children in her family, and her father could not afford the college, but my mother would never let anything stop her when she had her mind set. She was just a kid herself, a teenager, but here she was, living away from home and working while attending college. She was that kind of woman.

Mom may have had to work to pay her room and board, and it may have been tough finding enough time to study so she could make excellent grades, but I also think she had time to thoroughly enjoy college life. I have looked through a couple of her college yearbooks and a book of photographs taken with an old Kodak box camera during her years at Dakota Wesleyan. Both the yearbooks and photographs reflect lots of friends and lots of fun. Mom belonged to several organizations and clubs, both academic and social. She played roles in some of the university's dramatic productions.

In perusing Mom's college yearbooks, I also learned that she had been quite an athlete at Dakota Wesleyan. I was particularly impressed with a picture of her running the hurdles. I said, "Mom, you look great in that picture."

Mom smiled and said to me with mock indignation, "Young man, I'll have you know that at the time that picture was taken, my measurements were exactly the same as the measurements of Miss America that year!"

One of Mother's friends at Dakota Wesleyan was Francis Case, who later represented South Dakota in the United States Congress from 1937 until his death in 1962. He spent the years 1937 to 1950 in the House of Representatives and 1951 to 1962 in the Senate. I remember being with Mother one day when she was campaigning for the office of Todd County superintendent of schools, and she crossed trails with Francis Case someplace out on the prairie. He was campaigning for the first of his terms in the House of Representatives. During their conversation, Mom mentioned that I enjoyed reading military books and that I thought I would like to go to West Point someday. Senator Case told me, "Billy, you study hard, and if I am still in Congress when you graduate from high school, I'll see to it that you have an appointment to West Point."

Not only was Francis Case still in Congress when I graduated from high school, he was still in Washington, D.C., when

I took Mom and Dorothy Jo back there on a sightseeing trip in about 1955. Senator Case made sure we saw and did everything a tourist should see and do in Washington. With apologies to the Washington Monument, the Lincoln Memorial, et cetera, one of the highlights of our journey was having a bowl of the famous Senate bean soup with Senator Case in the Senate Dining Room.

• • •

After Mother finished college, she again set out on her own and became a high school teacher in White River, South Dakota. She really had a love and respect for education, and that is something she instilled in me from a very early age. I was not around yet, but later I heard stories about some of the remarkable things my mother had done during these early years. For example, while she was teaching in White River, the great worldwide flu epidemic struck in 1918. In addition to her teaching duties, my mother also nursed people all around White River, South Dakota.

Not many people today are aware of the danger and the damage of the flu epidemic of 1918. Unlike the recent versions of the flu, this was nothing to be held off by an inoculation. More than 28 percent of the U.S. population contracted the flu, and it killed 2.5 percent of its victims. What did this mean in terms of historical impact? To quote Gina Kolata's excellent book *Flu* (Farrar, Straus, Giroux, 1999): "The epidemic affected the course of history and was a terrifying presence at the end of World War I, killing more Americans in a single year than had died in battle in World War I, World War II, the Korean War, and the Vietnam War combined."

My mother opened a clinic in White River with beds for twelve people. At a time when entire towns were wiped out by the flu, she faithfully brought medical attention to everyone in or near White River. She helped people all over the county, out on the farms, in the small villages, everywhere. In some instances on farms, she found people with the flu living in mud huts and lying in an inch of fetid water.

My mother had at one time wanted to be a doctor, but medical school was out of the question, so she studied biology and taught biology in school. She had learned about medicine as well, and later she would say during that whole epidemic, she never lost a patient. She was very proud of that, as well she should be. It is an incredible record considering that more than an estimated one hundred million people died of this terrible scourge worldwide. For more than fifty years after the epidemic, Mother received letters of thanks from people she had nursed.

. . .

It was during that period in 1918 to 1919 that my mother met my father. Byron Barker was a rugged outdoor kind of guy, an adventurous man who had grown up on a ranch in South Dakota with cattle and horses. He was working in the electrical industry when he met my mother. Electricity was in its infancy then. It was quite a pioneering and exciting time for the field. He and my mother married in 1920, and Mom accompanied him on various jobs. After a year and a half or so, my father became foreman on the high line through the state of Washington. They were living in a tent city near a little town called Darrington when I arrived. The tent city was created because this was still the Wild West. There simply were no towns near the rugged area where the electric lines were being installed. I was born on December 12, 1923. They went to a doctor's house in Darrington where my mother gave birth, and a few days later they returned with me to the tent city. Mom said, "It was a perfect place for an Indian father and his papoose."

One early evening while my father was working on the high line in Washington, a problem developed high on a tower. All of my father's men had left for the day, so he decided to handle the problem himself. Unfortunately, his "hooks"— which are spiked climbing irons used by linemen to provide footholds—were not at the tower, but several pairs belonging to the men who worked for my father were located. Although they didn't fit him perfectly, my father selected a pair and climbed the tower. But the hooks slipped. My father came crashing down and sustained an injury to his hip joint that affected his spine in a manner that proved fatal six years later.

In spite of his tragic accident, my father and mother were smitten with the state of Washington—so much so that when my father's responsibilities on the high line were completed, he signed on for another job in Seattle. My mother said, "The tent city was a lot of fun, but I was ready for an apartment in Seattle."

• • •

About this time, in 1924, my mother's father, my grandfather Robert E. Tarleton, the minister, died back in South Dakota. My mother had younger sisters and a brother, so there were still two daughters and a young son at home with my grandmother, but she was now a widow, living in South Dakota. She decided she was going to southwest Missouri. It had actually been a dream of my grandparents to retire on a farm in Missouri, and now my grandmother was determined to do as she and my grandfather had planned. She bought a farm in Houston, Missouri. She was a strong-willed independent woman, just like my mother.

The idea of her mother alone with her younger sisters and a brother on a farm in Missouri did not sit well with my mother. She and my father were both concerned about this arrangement. After a short while, my mother and father moved from Washington and went down to Missouri to help my grandmother and try to make this farm work. After a while, they convinced her that she was not cut out for farming, and my grandmother traded the farm for a house in Springfield, Missouri. My grandmother, ever enterprising, opened a grocery store down the street from her house. My mother and father stayed there with her for a short time, but my father was still working electrical jobs near Springfield and then in Texas and in Mexico.

• • •

Soon we moved to Pampa, Texas, and then to Brownsville, Texas, right on the border. My father would go across the border every day, where he was foreman on a job installing lines in Mexico. It was just across the Rio Grande in a town called Matamoros. I was still just a small child then, around four or five years old. I guess you could say I absorbed a certain amount of traveling in my blood because of my parents and their willingness to follow electrical jobs wherever they led.

There definitely was a pioneering spirit in those days. People did what they had to do for work and for family.

As a side note, I have a vivid memory from that Texas period of when there was a visit by Charles Lindbergh to the airport in Brownsville. He made his historic flight across the Atlantic Ocean in 1927, so this was some time shortly after that. It made a powerful impression on me, because I can still remember it to this day. My mom and dad took me out to the airport, and my dad put me on his shoulders so I could see Lindbergh and all the hoopla. It was an unforgettable thrill for me.

• • •

After Texas, our family moved back to Springfield in 1928, again to be with my grandmother, and my father had a good job there. He had been appointed electrical inspector for the city of Springfield, and he went out to buy a new car because there would be a lot of driving in his work. He never worked a day as inspector. He was supposed to start on a Monday, and he became ill on the prior Friday. He was never well again. He died thirteen weeks later. The crushed hip had never healed properly, and ultimately it had rubbed up against his spine. As best as the medical profession could tell in those days, that is what killed him.

My father died at home. I remember that I was sitting on my grandmother's lap. She was reading me the funnies from the newspaper. My mother came out of the bedroom and over to me, and she said, "Billy, Daddy has gone up to live with Jesus." I was only six years old, but I understood he had died. The manner in which my mother chose to tell me was beautiful.

There was no crying, no hysterics, even though she herself had suffered this terrible loss. I was too young to realize it at the time, but with her gentleness and tenderness and by painting the picture that way for me, my mother had made the loss of my father more bearable for me.

Never in the ensuing weeks did my mother ever cry in front of me. I am sure she cried alone, but she never cried in front of me, never lamented her fate. She just said to me that she and I were going to be partners, and this was going to work. It was 1929—the Depression had arrived and she was a young widow with a six-year-old son.

My mother raised me on her own from the time I was six years old until I was thirteen, through the Great Depression and during the dust bowl in South Dakota. Those are very formative years. She would later remarry, but there was a long stretch of years when aside from some extended family, it was just her and me. Our bond, which was already strong, became even stronger.

Although I was just a child at the time, I immediately recognized author Timothy Egan's eloquent descriptions of the dust bowl when I read his book *The Worst Hard Time* (Houghton Mifflin, 2006):

Earlier, the land had been overturned in a great speculative frenzy to make money in an unsustainable wheat market. After a big run-up, prices crashed. The rains disappeared—not just for a season but for years on end. With no sod to hold the earth in place, the soil calcified and started to blow. Dust clouds boiled up, ten thousand feet or more in the sky; and rolled like moving mountains—a force of their own. When the dust fell, it penetrated everything: hair, nose, throat, kitchen, bed-room, well. A scoop shovel was needed just to clean the house in the morning. The eeriest thing was the dark-ness. People tied themselves to ropes before going to a barn just a few hundred feet away; like a walk in space, tethered to the life support center. Chickens roosted in midafternoon.

Mother and I experienced the misery of the dust bowl be-cause after my father died, my mother turned to what she knew—teaching. She looked for a teaching job around Spring-field and other nearby communities, but times were hard then and jobs were scarce. I can still remember the time she came home from an interview, and she said the superintendent of the school told her that she was qualified and that he had been im-pressed with her résumé. Then he told her that he had to give the job to a man because the man had a family to support.

And my mother said, "I am a woman and I, too, have a fam-ily to support."

No luck.

After that she wrote to my father's older brother, who lived in Mission, South Dakota, and told him the situation. He got her a job teaching at Mission High School, and that's why we moved to South Dakota. She was qualified and an excellent teacher. And she made the most of the opportunity. That was another thing she taught me, just an incredible work ethic—a resilient but steady march forward in the face of obstacles.

Her college acting experience paid off in her teaching ca-reer. Mom directed plays both in White River and Mission.

Those White River productions were before my time, but I had the best seats in the house when the Mission students trod the boards under Mom's direction. The Mission High School plays were staged in the gymnasium at the Indian boarding school west of Mission, and the young actors played to full houses nightly—Friday and Saturday nights, that is. Monday through Friday the actors had to concentrate on their studies.

After she taught at the high school for two years, she became the principal of the school, and then she ran for political office and became the Todd County superintendent of schools. She also wrote an excellent history text about South Dakota, *Our State,* which was used throughout the school system from the 1930s to the early 1960s. When I was hosting Miss USA, Miss South Dakotas frequently told me that they had studied *Our State* in school.

• • •

I attended school in South Dakota from the second grade up through the eighth grade, and it was a marvelous education. I never had my mother for a teacher, but she always checked my homework. She was always teaching me, guiding me, and stressing the importance of education. There was never any question of me going to college. It was just naturally assumed. She talked about my grammar school work as preparation for college. She always encouraged me in everything I tried to do.

The respect and tradition of education that my mother established paid off in every aspect of my life. I learned to love reading from an early age because before I could read, she read to me. She got me a set of those classic children's stories called Journeys Through Bookland that I still have. I loved to have her read to me and to this day—and I am eighty-four years old—I love reading. My appreciation of reading and books all came from her. She read to me until I learned to read.

Surprisingly, the best thing that ever happened to me in terms of education was to get out of the first grade in Springfield, Missouri, and go up to South Dakota, where all the children in first, second, third, and fourth grades were in one room. Next door, the fifth, sixth, seventh, and eighth grades were in another room. The moment I got there, my reading and learning took off—with my mother's help of course.

I had just started the first grade in Springfield, Missouri, about the time my father died. First grade was when you began to learn to read and write in the public schools of that era. It was my misfortune that the Springfield school system was experimenting at that time with their version of John Dewey's progressive education. When I was learning to read in the first grade, we did not have phonics at all. We did not worry about the sound of letters. *T* was a man with a hat on, *N* was a haystack, *M* was two haystacks, and so on. I could look at the word *table* and I would not know whether it was a table or window or door. My mother would ask, "What is the sound of that word?" I did not know anything about the sounds.

As soon as I got to South Dakota and that two-room schoolhouse, we were using phonics and my reading ability took off immediately. It was wonderful. There was also an Episcopal church with a library in the basement, and that library became my playground on many a cold winter day. Those cold winters up in South Dakota would include blizzards that shut down the school. So naturally, I stayed home and read. Sometimes there were two or three days in a row when you could not go to school because of the blizzards, and I would read some more. Had I stayed in Springfield with that nonphonics progressive education, I do not know if I would ever have learned to read.

In addition to reading, my mother taught me how to drive. I remember she had a two-door Chevrolet when I was probably around eleven or twelve years old. I would drive it out on the highway occasionally, with Mom tensely watching my every move. In those days, there were no paved roads in South Dakota. The highways were all gravel, and they would leave a ridge down the middle, so if you were going to pass someone or go around, you had to carefully cross that little ridge. She never really lost her temper with me, but one time I found the car in front of her office with the key in the ignition—not unusual in Mission—and I decided to go for a little spin. Mother came out of her office just as I returned, and she was displeased, to put it mildly. I chose not to do that again.

My mother eventually met my stepfather, Louis Valandra, while we were living in South Dakota. I was thirteen by then, and they got married. He was a kind man to both me and my mother. I got along very well with him. He and my mother had a son, my half brother, Kent. My brother and I immediately bonded, and we have been friends for a lifetime. He is fourteen years younger than I am, but we have always had good times together. When they were married, I had just finished the eighth grade, and we moved back to Springfield, Missouri, in 1937 so that my mother could be close to her mother. My stepfather went into the tire business there. I lived at home until I was nineteen. After that I joined the navy, and soon thereafter married Dorothy Jo.

• • •

My mother taught me so many things, it would be impossible to list them all. I would like to think I inherited her strong work ethic. I certainly did my fair share of traveling and some risk taking, as did she. She gave me a love of reading and a reverence for education. In her lifetime, she displayed a never-ending tenderness and affection for her mother and her family, which had a profound influence on me. She lost my father early, and she endured. I lost Dorothy Jo far too early, and I believe Mom's strength helped me endure that loss. She shared her sense of humor with me, which no doubt helped develop one in me, and that humor served me well in my career. She took care of me when there was nobody else. Later on, I took care of her.

My mother lived to be ninety-one years old. She lived with me in my home in Hollywood for many years before and after Dorothy Jo had passed away. She was a part of my life for over sixty-five years. In the end, things had come full circle. She fell when she was eighty-nine years old and shattered her wrist. Following surgery, she had a stroke. After the stroke, Mother was confined to a wheelchair and required nurses twenty-four hours a day. I had an elevator installed so the nurses could take Mother downstairs and out among the flowers she loved.

We remained close all through life. How could we not? We had been close from the very beginning and from the years when it was just the two of us. In tent cities, on an Indian reservation in South Dakota, in small towns in Texas and Missouri, in snowbound freezing Dakota winters, and driving on dusty roads in a 1928 Chevrolet coupe with a rumble seat that she had when I was small. She lived to a good old age, saw almost all of the twentieth century, and died here in Hollywood. It was an incredible journey, and she was an amazing woman. She said we were going to be partners after my father died and things were going to be fine, and she was right. She made sure—with all her strength, tenderness, and intelligence—that things did turn out fine. Blessed, to be sure.

Up, Up, and Away as a
Naval Aviation Cadet

Today we look back and say that World War II was the last of the popular wars, and it is true. No one had any trouble making up his mind who was right and who was wrong in that war. I was a freshman at Drury College (a university now) in Springfield, Missouri, when Pearl Harbor was attacked. Immediately, just about every young man in the country was ready to enlist in the military.

The most popular subject of conversation among the boys at Drury was which branch of the service we were going to join. Some went into the U.S. Marines; some opted for the Army Air Corps, as it was called then; others chose the Coast Guard. And so it went.

Me, I decided to become a naval aviator. Now I had never

seen the ocean. I had never even been up in an airplane. And I certainly had never given any thought whatsoever to what was involved with landing an airplane on a carrier.

· · ·

My decision to become a naval aviator was strictly a matter of vanity. One day I was paging through a glossy magazine and saw a full-page picture of a young, handsome naval aviator leaning against a sleek fighter plane. He was wearing his white dress uniform, the one with gold buttons, shoulder boards, a high collar, and a white hat with gold braid. Of course, his wings of gold were pinned prominently over his heart—and to top it all off, he had a deep tan. He was one terrific-looking guy.

I took a long look at the picture of that great-looking naval aviator, and I thought, "If I am going to war, I want to go to war looking like that guy." I went down to the post office that day and signed up to become a naval aviation cadet. When I finally had my wings of gold and my fighter plane, I used to go out and lean against it occasionally. Unfortunately, there was never a photographer around.

I wasn't commissioned as an ensign in the United States Navy until two and a half years after I enlisted because the navy ordered me to remain at Drury for my sophomore year. You had to have completed two years of college to qualify to become a naval aviation cadet. I reported for active duty on June 9, 1943.

The navy training regimen was pretty intense, but it was also a lot of fun. Over the course of eighteen months, I trained at eight different bases, met all kinds of different people, made new friends, and flew eight different airplanes, including the legendary Corsair. We worked hard, but we all wanted to be there. I don't mean to imply that World War II was fun for anybody. I'm just saying I loved flying, and I enjoyed the camaraderie of the navy.

. . .

My navy training began at William Jewell College in Liberty, Missouri, just outside of Kansas City. The first part of the cadet training was all ground school and athletics. We put in hours and hours of physical activity, conditioning, and sports. We were all young men in pretty good condition, but I'm talking four hours of hard-core physical training during June, July, and August in Missouri. We did all this rigorous conditioning and athletic activity in the heat of the sweltering, humid summer. On breaks, we lined up at the drinking fountain, and guys would be yelling from the back, "You've had enough. Move on." Sometimes they were not so good-natured.

We played basketball, wrestled, boxed, did gymnastics, and ran track. Four hours a day of athletics and four hours of ground school. I never sweated so much in my life. Track was a particularly new experience for me. The navy had what was called military track. One day our platoon was scheduled to compete with another platoon in the quarter mile. Now, if you know anything about track, you know that the quarter mile is a tough race—that and the half mile—because you have to run fast the whole time. And a quarter mile is a long way to go. I had no experience in track and had never run a quarter mile in my life, but the physical training officer picked me out from our platoon and another guy out from the other platoon and told us to race each other.

"On your marks. Get set. Go." I knew nothing about pacing or anything about running technique; I just took off, not as fast as I could, but fast enough to be in the lead. I was still ahead of the other cadet about halfway around the track, maybe a little more. Soon, however, he sped by me. I tried to keep up with him, but I couldn't. Pretty soon I was running as fast as I could to catch this fellow, and something happened that had never happened to me before: black started coming from the top and the bottom of my eyes. My vision was slowly closing down, and I realized that I was about to pass out. So I slowed down, and I could see more. As soon as I started running hard again, the black in my eyes returned. I was very close to passing out, but I kept running. Finally, I finished the quarter mile. He beat me, of course, and the men in my platoon were commiserating. I wasn't concerned about losing. I was concerned about surviving. Then I found out that this cadet was the high school quarter-mile champion of Kansas. I was running the quarter mile for the first time in my life, and my competitor was the state champion. The guys in the platoon all had a good laugh about that. They thought it was hilarious. I considered it a near-death experience.

I was a member of the Sixth Battalion at William Jewell. Soon after our arrival, our battalion was addressed at some length by a gentleman whose name was Mason. As I recall, he was a lieutenant, and he was a very good speaker. His speaking ability is probably the reason he was given the assignment to sell us war bonds.

He told us what fine young men we were to have volunteered to become naval aviators, that our assignment would be one of the most important in winning the war in the Pacific, et cetera, et cetera.

"But," Lieutenant Mason added, "I want to ask you to do even more for your country. I want each of you cadets to sign up to buy a war bond every month." Then he explained in great detail why war bonds were so important to winning the war. After holding us transfixed for several minutes with his war bond pitch, Lieutenant Mason said, "In conclusion, gentlemen, I think I should tell you that I am in charge of all weekend liberty at this base and I take my job very seriously."

We laughed, but we all bought war bonds.

. . .

About two months later, another officer, a commander, spoke to the Sixth Battalion on a subject that would deeply affect the lives of many cadets in the battalion. It was in this speech that the Great Purge reared its ugly head for the first time. It wasn't mentioned as such, but the Great Purge is what it came to be called.

You talk with any cadet of my era, and they all know about the purge. Basically, when I originally signed up to become a naval aviator, you were given nine months of training as a cadet, and if successful, you got your wings. If you washed out, you went back to civilian life so you could join the Army Air Corps, the merchant marines, the U.S. marines, or whatever you wanted to do. While I was at William Jewell, the navy changed all that and gave us a chance to get out. Anybody who wanted to could get out immediately, but if you stayed in and you washed out later, you went to the Great Lakes and became a sailor. You didn't have the opportunity to go choose something else. I'll never forget it.

The commander encouraged us to stay in the cadet program, of course. He said, "You're the cream of the crop. We haven't had a better battalion come through here than you. You are not going to wash out. Don't leave the navy now. You came into the navy because you wanted to fly for the navy. You will fly for the navy. You stay with it."

All but one cadet in the battalion did stay, but later on, during the purge, probably 25 percent washed out, maybe more. The navy didn't lose as many pilots in the Pacific as they thought they were going to lose, and now they had more pilots than they needed. I talked with instructors after the war who told me they had been forced to wash out a percentage of their cadets, even though the instructors thought the cadets were qualified to continue in the program.

So to get your wings after I got in the navy, you had to be able to fly and you had to do well in ground school, but it also helped to have lady luck on your shoulder. I was a good pilot; I worked hard and did well in ground school, but I was also lucky. I got my coveted wings of gold in spite of the purge, and though some cadets in my class had hairy crashes and some were killed, I was never in an accident or suffered injury.

• • •

My first taste of flying came at the next training base, which was in Ames, Iowa, at Iowa State University. We had ground school and athletics at that location also, but at last, we did a little flying. We had civilian flight instructors, and my first one was a fellow named Mr. Shivers. I thought the name was appropriate because he was liable to be shivering with me at the controls of an airplane for the first time. He must have gotten very nervous because one morning I came out to the airport and Mr. Shivers was gone. My new instructor was a very attractive young lady. I approved of the trade. I can't remember her name, but she took me up, up, and away in a canvas plane called a Taylorcraft.

Mr. Shivers had familiarized me with the controls and the basics of flying before he suddenly bailed out. Apparently, my new instructor thought I was about ready to solo because she emphasized emergency landings in our first couple of flights together. Undoubtedly, her thought was that before she sent Cadet Barker up alone, it was her responsibility to prepare him to get back down safely in case the engine of his Taylorcraft conked out. I learned that in an emergency, the pilot should immediately spot a place on the ground where it would be as safe as possible to land his plane.

Now, my instructor didn't tell me what I am about to write. She didn't even hint at it. This was my own idea: If I were flying over a forest or a city, finding a place to land an airplane in an emergency could indeed pose a problem, but because I was flying over Iowa, it was no problem. There were excellent landing fields in every direction. In fact, that's all there were—beautiful open fields. Besides, I had a backup position. We always wore parachutes, and parachutes are for jumping. Jumping was exactly what I would do if there was a really serious problem. Let the airplane get down on its own!

In any event, the fateful day for my solo flight arrived. An instructor doesn't tell a student, "Tomorrow you'll solo." The poor student probably wouldn't get a wink of sleep. The ac-

cepted way for an instructor to solo a student is to take the student up for a routine lesson, at the same time checking to see if
the would-be soloist is behaving in a reasonably sane manner
that day. If the cadet's behavior justifies the risk, the instructor has the cadet return to the airfield, where the instructor
gets out of the airplane, and almost casually but with an air of
complete confidence, tells the future ace, "OK, take it around
by yourself."

That is precisely what my instructor did. When she said,
"Take it around by yourself," she meant for me to take off,
fly once around the field in the landing pattern, and land the
plane, hopefully without unpleasant incident.

I'm delighted to report that I did my instructor proud. As I
was flying, I thought: "Here I am, a nineteen-year-old kid who
had never been up in an airplane until a few weeks ago, and
now I am up here flying this thing all by myself. The United
States Navy has worked a miracle." I was elated.

I made a nice three-point landing, navy style, taxied to the
hangar, shut off the engine, jumped out of the plane, and gave
my instructor a big kiss right on the lips. It was a lot more fun
than kissing Mr. Shivers would have been.

* * *

After learning to fly a Taylorcraft at Iowa State University, I
headed south for the University of Georgia and what the navy
called preflight school. At preflight we put flying aside again
and concentrated on ground school and physical conditioning.
Our day was to consist of four hours of books and four hours
of bruises. But, as I shall explain, I lucked out.

The navy had four preflight schools in the United States: the

University of Georgia, where I went; St. Mary's in California; the University of Iowa (not to be confused with Iowa State University, where I soloed); and the University of North Carolina. These preflight schools were notorious throughout the navy for being tough, both in the ground school and in physical training—particularly the physical training program.

Both at William Jewell and Iowa State University, the athletic instructors had warned us that if we thought it was tough with them, just wait until we got to preflight school, and it was to preflight that aviation cadet Robert W. Barker was headed. Was I quaking in my boots? No, not quite . . . but almost.

We studied everything from engines to navigation to airplane identification in preflight. They wanted us to be able to identify all the different kinds of airplanes in the enemy's arsenal. We also had to study all the American aircraft as well. The navy considered it bad form to shoot down your own planes. The curriculum was quite intense. For example, to train us in identifying aircraft quickly, the instructor flashed a picture of a plane on a screen and we had to instantly identify it in a fraction of a second. It was thorough and professional training. We studied meteorology, navigation, engines, Morse code. You name it. We studied it.

But the most demanding part of preflight was not ground school, it was the athletic program, and the most grueling part of the athletic program was said to be the obstacle course. The course incorporated all kinds of physical rigors—not just running, but acrobatics, tumbling, crawling, climbing, scaling, jumping, and more running. It was brutal.

Now, you will recall I indicated that I had lucked out. Well, let me explain. When I got to preflight school in Georgia, they had tryouts for the preflight basketball team. All branches of the service had athletic teams, and they were an important part of morale. I had played basketball all my life, so I tried out and was selected for the team. I could hardly believe my ears when I was told that playing on the basketball team meant that I avoided all other athletic training, including the dreaded obstacle course. I went to ground school for four hours a day and I played basketball four hours a day. Just too sweet! Unfortunately, as irony had it, in our first scrimmage, I went up for a rebound, came down on another player's foot, and severely sprained my ankle. It popped so loudly that everyone thought it was broken. I had been playing basketball since I was seven years old and never sprained an ankle before, but this was really a bad sprain. I was in the hospital for three days, and my leg was black-and-blue almost to my knee.

When I got out, my ankle was still too bad for me to march with my platoon. I had to join the crippled platoon. This was a group of cadets with broken arms, broken collarbones, separated shoulders, and every other injury known to man. Still unable to play on the basketball team, I ended up shooting free throws for four hours a day. As you can imagine, I got to be a pretty good free throw shooter, but one day the coach came to me and said, "Look, Barker, you're not helping the team. If that ankle isn't better and you can't play, I'm going to have to send you back to the platoon."

That meant the obstacle course. Fear is a great motivator: I said, "I can run, Coach. I can play." And to demonstrate to the coach, I started racing up and down the gym. I practiced from that day forward. Miraculous healing started right then and there. I am still one of the few cadets from World War II who can tell you he never saw the obstacle course at preflight. I will always be grateful to basketball.

• • •

With each step in our progressive cadet training, we gained more knowledge and flight experience. After preflight, I went to Millington Naval Air Station just outside of Memphis, Tennessee, where we really got into flight training, including night and formation flying. At the Memphis base, we were trained to fly the Stearman, which was a biplane—upper wing and a lower wing and an open cockpit. It looked like an old World War I fighter plane. They were great airplanes. I always said if I ever had an airplane, that would be the one I wanted to own.

The Stearman was called the yellow peril because it had a very narrow landing gear. If you came in for a landing and you weren't lined up well with the wind, the wind would lift one wing so high that you would scrape the opposite wingtip on the ground, but you could really have fun in those planes. You could do acrobatics. You could loop it. You could do almost anything with that plane, but you couldn't fly it upside down because the carburetor cut out.

• • •

After Memphis, my next stop was the huge naval air station at Corpus Christi, Texas. Corpus Christi was a vast complex of airfields, and if the wash-out monster didn't tap me on the shoulder, it would be at Corpus Christi where I would complete my flight training, be commissioned as an ensign, have the commanding officer pin my wings of gold on my chest, be assigned to fighters, get leave, go home, and marry Dorothy Jo. All in that order.

Getting my wings and being assigned to fighters were certainly important to me, but my ultimate goal was to make Dorothy Jo my bride. I had looked forward to having Dorothy Jo become Mrs. Bob Barker since our first date six years before when we listened to Ella Fitzgerald sing "A-Tisket, A-Tasket" at the Shrine Mosque in Springfield. We wrote to each other regularly, and I called her frequently. Every letter and call was filled with "when you get your wings" plans. These were not detailed wedding plans. Actually, we never bothered with those. It was just a matter of "we'll get married." And we did.

• • •

But before that, the next step was what the navy called basic training. "After all the training I had already had," I thought, "are we only now getting down to basics?" I was assigned to Cabaniss Field for basic, and this phase of our training concentrated more on flying and less on everything else. Not only were we flying more, we were flying in our biggest airplane yet, the BT-13. It had a retractable cockpit hood and retractable landing gear—wheels, that is. And woe be to the cadet who forgets to pull up his wheels after takeoff. Or even worse—much worse—the cadet who forgets to put down his wheels before landing.

Takeoffs and landings are considered emergencies. Bad things can happen, and when they do, you want to get out of the airplane fast. Hence, the cockpit hood is retracted on takeoffs and landings and closed in flight. After checking out in the BT-13, we decided that we might not be hot pilots as yet, but we were certainly getting warmer. In a month or two, we were completely comfortable at the controls of a BT-13, takeoffs, landings, formation flying, night flying, dogfighting, dive-bombing, acrobatics—we did it all. We were ready to move on, and move on we did.

Next, we went from all the good stuff I listed above—stuff that was genuinely fun for anyone who aspired to go to the fleet as a fighter pilot—to something new and mentally demanding: instrument flying. I was sent to the field at Beeville for my instrument training. At Beeville we flew the SNJ, an even more powerful plane than the BT-13. The SNJ was a trainer that was the next thing to a fighter. In fact, I understand that in some countries not as advanced as the United States in airpower, the SNJ was used as a fighter plane in combat.

In instrument training, the cadet closed a canvas hood over his cockpit, effectively blinding him to anything outside the cockpit. Of course, the instructor in the front cockpit was on the alert for other aircraft and prepared to prevent any catastrophe that the cadet under the hood might otherwise cause. The instruments we used were an airspeed indicator, altimeter, compass, and turn-and-bank indicator. With the turn-and-bank indicator, we could determine whether we were flying straight and level. If we weren't straight and level, the turn-and-bank indicator would show us which way we were banking and how steeply.

These instruments are very basic and simple, and can serve you very well. However, if a cadet misreads them or fails to give them his full attention while under the canvas hood, these instruments can send the cadet to the Great Lakes, washed out. It happened to many a would-be ace.

• • •

Advanced training was next, and supposedly it was the last hurdle before graduation—more about that a bit later. I went to Waldron Field for advanced, and it was more of the good stuff, including dogfighting, this time flying the SNJ. It was at advanced that I received a compliment I have savored all of my life.

Robert L. Voight, from Nebraska, was an exemplary cadet who excelled in ground school, flying, physical training—the works. He and I were selected to go up and dogfight one day—and did we ever get it on. Both of us tried every trick we had been taught and some we improvised. When we came down, our flight suits were drenched with perspiration and we were exhausted. Voight said, "Bob, you are the best I have ever fought."

"I was about to tell you that you are the best I ever fought," I replied. Coming from a cadet for whom I had so much respect, it was a compliment I shall always remember.

• • •

I finished advanced training and was ready to graduate, go home, and get married. Right? Wrong. Earlier I explained that the navy had not lost as many pilots as they had expected, so the cadet program had been lengthened. Well, when we finished advanced training, we were informed that the program had been lengthened again.

We were sent to the main station for what was hastily dubbed preoperational training. The good part about preoperational was that we checked out in the SBD dive-bomber, one of the most famous navy planes of World War II. It was SBD pilots who sank four Japanese carriers at the Battle of Midway, the turning point of the war in the Pacific.

We didn't do any dive-bombing. We just went up and flew around the countryside for a few weeks, and at long last, the order came to prepare for graduation. Man, was I prepared! I got to a telephone as soon as I could and called Dorothy Jo. I told her that there weren't going to be any more delays. I was going to become Ensign Robert W. Barker and she was going to become Mrs. Bob Barker.

· · ·

I have told you the story of our elopement; now my bride accompanied me when I reported for operational training at the naval air station in DeLand, Florida. At DeLand, I flew the FM-2 fighter, which I have already described as an improved version of the much acclaimed F4F Wildcat. We were commissioned officers now, proudly wearing our hard-earned wings of gold, and we concentrated on flying and more flying. There was no more physical training or ground school. We were full-fledged naval aviators, and our next stop would be the fleet. As fighter pilots, our principal responsibility would be to shoot down enemy airplanes, with some strafing of enemy ground targets and ships thrown in.

In operational training we did more of all the things we had learned along the way: lots of formation flying, night flying, and dogfighting. But operational training also included gunnery flights—firing live ammunition at a sleeve towed by one of the pilots in our flight—and field carrier landings. Naval aviators practice field carrier landings for hours and hours before they do the real thing.

Field carrier landings are just what the name implies: a carrier deck is chalked out on a field in the same way a football field is done in chalk. Pilots fly a pattern around the field carriers, exactly as they will around a real carrier, and they are brought in for a landing by a landing signal officer, just exactly as they will be on a carrier. By the time we were sent up to the Great Lakes Naval Air Station to do our twelve qualifying carrier landings on the Wolverine (a carrier kept at Lake Michigan for just that purpose), we were ready. Every pilot in my flight qualified, and I am proud to say that I was one of those who received a grade of superior.

• • •

When I finished operational training at DeLand, I fully expected orders assigning me to a seagoing squadron, but as you will recall, I was among the cadets who had to survive the purge necessitated by a surplus of naval aviators. The purge was not a pleasant experience. But what was about to happen to me next would be very pleasant, the most pleasant experience of my two and a half years in the navy. I received orders assigning me to fighter affiliation at what is today Cape Kennedy in Florida. During World War II, it was Banana River Naval Air Station.

Upon reading my orders, Dorothy Jo asked, "What is fighter affiliation?"

I replied honestly, "I have no idea."

I managed to find out that Banana River was a big—really big—Mariner base, and that there were many, many Mariners flying out of Banana River. But the Mariner was a huge four-engine seaplane. Why would I, a fighter pilot, be going to a Mariner base? As long as they were stationed at a base on the east coast of Florida, the Mariners would hardly need fighter protection.

When we arrived at Banana River, I and six other gloriously happy ensigns who had just finished operational learned that we were to be the only seven fighter pilots on the base and that our sole responsibility was to fly out over the beautiful Atlantic and make gunnery runs on Mariners. The crews of the Mariners would fire at us with cameras, in preparation for firing at enemy fighters with machine guns. Fighter pilots love making gunnery runs. We loved fighter affiliation. Dorothy Jo could be with me and I loved Dorothy Jo, too. It was a lovefest.

Snug Harbor was our home at Banana River. It was what folks used to call a tourist court, and Dorothy Jo got cabins for us and for Howard Hessick and his bride. Snug Harbor was on the Indian River, complete with a pier, on which Dorothy Jo got a lovely tan, and a sailboat, which Howard sailed downriver and then had to have towed back. Fortunately, Howard was a much better fighter pilot than he was a sailor. Dorothy Jo and I used to go to Miami, which was a very exciting place during World War II, filled with uniforms of every description. We made trips into the fascinating swamps. I even got Dorothy Jo off the pier long enough to go to the beach.

Of course, I had to spend a few hours on the flight line every day, not necessarily flying. We played a lot of hearts. If you had a good hand and your name was called to give a Mariner a bad time, one of the other pilots was always happy to pretend to shoot down that seaplane. Fighter affiliation was the good life, there's no doubt about it. But as a comedian might say: Seriously, folks, I think I was a better fighter pilot as a result of that duty. I think all those gunnery runs on Mariners improved my skills to the extent that I was better prepared for combat, and it's a good thing that I felt better prepared for combat because my stay at Banana River was about to become history.

The commanding officer of the base learned that we, the seven gloriously happy fighter pilots, had not been to sea. He ordered that we be shipped out. It seems that the commanding officer thought this soft berth of fighter affiliation should be a reward for fighter pilots who had been to sea and earned it. Who's to blame him? He was right. That's why he was the commanding officer of the base.

The first pilot to arrive from the fleet was Jack Lyon, a likable lieutenant, who was followed by Wally Maya, an equally likable marine captain, who had flown in Pappy Boyington's Black Sheep Squadron, so you know he was a character. I got to know Jack and Wally well enough for Dorothy Jo and me to go out to dinner with them a couple of times before I, to use the commanding officer's expression, "shipped out."

• • •

I had known the joy of fighter affiliation for about two months when I received orders to report to Grosse Ile Naval Air Station in Michigan, where I would be placed in a fighter pilot pool to await assignment to a seagoing squadron.

When Jack Lyon learned that I was about to depart, he felt compelled, as an officer and a gentleman, to bid Dorothy Jo farewell. Not in person, however—in his plane. I wasn't there. I was at the base, but Dorothy Jo described it to me later. She was in our cabin packing and talking with the landlady, who was helping her to get packed. There was a big wooden water tower near our Snug Harbor cabin. She said suddenly they heard an airplane that sounded as if it were headed directly for our cabin. She said that they could hear it getting closer and closer.

The landlady started to panic and began screaming that the plane was cracking up, that it was going to crash right into the cabin. Indeed, Jack was roaring right for the cabin. By this time, the landlady and Dorothy Jo were on their hands and knees crawling toward the door. Jack came barreling down right over them and pulled up at the last minute. He was so close that his slipstream pulled boards off the water tower near the cabin. (I was on the floor laughing when Dorothy Jo told me this story.) The landlady crawled out the door and cursed at Jack, called him a son of a blank, and promised to turn him in. Of course, she couldn't turn him in. She couldn't possibly get the number of the airplane before he was long gone.

The next day I went out to the base, and Jack said, "Did Dorothy Jo tell you I came by to say good-bye?"

I said, "She told me, and I loved it—but you will have to stay away from the landlady."

• • •

When we arrived in Michigan, Dorothy Jo worked another one of her patented miracles. She found a place to live within easy walking distance of the base. It was an enormous old frame home, and there were eleven fighter pilots and their wives living in every room that could possibly serve as a bedroom. We all had kitchen privileges.

I can understand why you might cringe to think about living under such conditions, but we were all young, we were all in love, and there was a war going on. And, best of all, when I looked up, all I could see was F4U Corsairs landing, taking off, and flying all over the sky. Grosse Ile was a Corsair base. I would go to sea in a Corsair squadron. I would be flying one of the finest fighters of World War II off a carrier in the Pacific. Not bad, particularly for a guy who had become a naval aviation cadet because he wanted to go to war looking like a naval aviator whose picture he had seen in a magazine.

But, folks, it was not to be. Oh, I checked out in the Corsair and had the thrill of logging a few hours in it. But I didn't go to sea. I will explain for you what happened, just as I explained it for members of *The Price Is Right* audience when someone asked what I did during World War II.

I was a naval aviator, a fighter pilot. I completed all facets of my training, including my qualifying landings on a carrier. I was all ready to go, and when the enemy heard that I was headed for the Pacific, they surrendered. That was the end of World War II.

Let Me Tell You of Dogs, Cats, Rabbits, and Ducks

For as long as I can remember, I have always loved animals and I have lived with them all of my life. Long before my "spay and neuter" sign-offs on *The Price Is Right* or my animal rights protests, I felt a special bond with numerous four-legged (and sometimes two-legged) friends. There is no doubt that the roots of my passionate feelings about animals began in these friendships, and because they have been important parts of my life, I want to share some of these friendships with you.

• • •

Although I honestly have no memory of the relationship, my mother showed me a photograph of me at age two or three and told me that I had a dog that I named Bo, who looks happy in the picture. My grandmother had a farm in Houston, Missouri, and I was living there with my mother, father, and Bo at the time the picture was shot. When I was six, soon after my father died, a neighbor gave me a puppy. I asked my mother if it would be all right if I named him Barney, which was the nickname many people gave my father. She said, "Yes, I think that Daddy would like that." So when Mom and I left Missouri for Mission, South Dakota, where she would teach, Barney went with us on the train. In Mission, when my mother was looking for me, she would go up on the roof of the hotel where we were living temporarily and look for the pack of dogs that I always had with me. That's how I checked on Barney, too. I usually spotted him out on the prairie at the edge of town, cavorting with his canine companions. Barney loved life in Mission.

. . .

Not too many years after I started hosting *The Price Is Right*, I acquired a dog in a most unusual manner. The front doorbell rang and I went to the door. When I opened it, there was a young lady standing there holding a puppy in her arms, just a baby dog.

She said, "I'm going home, back to Tennessee. I'm flying, and I can't take my little dog with me. It's so young they won't take it on the airplane."

"What are you going to do with it?" I asked her.

"I'm going to give it to you." And she handed me the dog.

I was absolutely astonished. All I could say was "OK."

I had never seen the girl before in my life, and I have never seen her since. But she handed me this baby dog. It had fleas, it was underweight, and the first thing I did was take it to the veterinarian. I asked him, "What kind of dog do you think this is?"

"I think it's probably a Chihuahua," he said. We named her Lupe, and she lived with Dorothy Jo and me for many years.

As Lupe began to grow—and she did grow considerably larger—it became apparent that she was more likely part whippet and maybe greyhound. After a few months, I took her back to the same vet and said, "Here's that Chihuahua that you identified for me when she was a puppy."

He looked at her and scratched his head and admitted, "Bob, I really missed on that one."

She actually grew so large that several times she jumped the six-foot fence behind my pool. She was graceful and beautiful to watch. As she bounded across the yard, she looked like a canine version of Bambi.

Another time, Dorothy Jo found a pair of little kittens in a brown paper bag in front of our house. Whoever left them at our door probably knew we loved animals. She brought them in the house and showed them to me.

"Aren't they darling?" she said.

And I said, "They certainly are. I'll see if I can't find them a home with someone at *The Price Is Right.*"

She said, "Too late. They already have a home right here."

They lived with us from then on. Dorothy Jo named them Gato and Tomas.

There was a time when we gave all of our animals Spanish names because we lived in this old Spanish house. One morning early, Dorothy Jo went out to get the paper, and there was Carlos. He was a long-legged German shepherd mix. He wasn't a puppy, but he was a young dog. Soon we discovered that he had seizures, which may have been why someone abandoned him. When he felt a seizure coming on, he would go to Dorothy Jo. He loved Dorothy Jo. She had a little desk in the utility room where she used to sit, and he would put his head on her lap while she was writing. She saved his life and he never forgot it. For the first few weeks he wouldn't leave her side. He followed her all over the house. When he started to have a seizure, he came to her and she would hold him.

We already had Carlos when that little girl delivered Lupe to us. Carlos loved Lupe from day one, and he never had another seizure after she arrived. It was totally inexplicable and totally fascinating. Carlos was having these seizures regularly until Lupe came into his life, and after he had her to take care of, he never had another seizure. The veterinarian had no explanation as to why that should have happened.

Carlos was unique in another respect. He liked to get up on top of the house. I talked with him several times about the dangers of his hobby, but he persisted. His MO was as follows: he went up the steps to the padre's walk that runs the length of the house, stepped up on a low built-in bench, and went out on the roof of our living room. The roof, typical of a Spanish home, is tile, rather steeply slanted, and the tile is definitely unsteady underfoot. Carlos, free spirit that he was, insisted on climbing up on the roof of the living room, sitting on his haunches, and surveying the neighborhood over the twelve-foot fence that surrounds our yard. Actually, he looked rather grand, even serene, on our rooftop, and he became a topic of conversation for the neighbors.

One day Carlos was on the roof and the doorbell rang. I

went to the door and found a friendly-looking stranger standing there with a look of utter amazement on his face. "Did you know that there is a dog sitting on your roof?"

"Certainly," I answered.

The stranger looked at me warily and said, "OK, I just wanted to be sure you knew that he was up there," as he backed away rapidly.

On another day, I was lying on a chaise by the pool, and Carlos was sitting on the roof as usual. Just as I was dozing off, I heard the sound I had dreaded, the sound of sliding tiles. I looked up just in time to see Carlos slide off the roof and fall about sixteen or seventeen feet to the brick patio. I jumped to my feet and rushed to Carlos, expecting the worst. He got to his feet with not a moan, groan, or whimper of any kind. With all the dignity he could muster, he simply walked away.

I told this story to a friend and he said, "That must have been a stupid dog."

I said, "Not at all. He never got on the roof again."

• • •

Many years before Carlos and Lupe joined our family, Mr. Baker, our basset hound, was mated with Doll Face, a lovely, provocative basset hound who made her home with our good friends Charlie and Shrimp Lyon. (At this point, allow me to take a break from the narrative to apologize to my animal rights friends for arranging to have my dog mated. It was a long time ago and I know better now, as I indicated time after time at the end of *The Price Is Right*. The only way to solve the tragic problem of animal overpopulation is to have your pets spayed or neutered.) Now, let us continue. Doll Face produced a beautiful, healthy litter of puppies. It had been agreed that Dorothy Jo and I would get our choice of the litter. After all, Mr. Baker had certainly done his part. Dorothy Jo chose a fine little fellow who had already been named Mr. Hubbard by Shrimp Lyon. When I asked Shrimp why she named him Mr. Hubbard, Shrimp said, "He just looked like Mr. Hubbard to me." That made sense to me.

Perhaps you are wondering how Shrimp got her own nickname. When she and Charlie were on one of their early dates, Charlie leaned down and kissed her and then said, "My, you're a little shrimp," and Shrimp she remained ever after.

Mr. Hubbard grew into a splendid representative of his breed. As he got older, he lost his hearing, but he got along quite well, even as an old dog. He just couldn't hear. We moved from Encino to our home in Hollywood in 1969, and in the process of moving in, the door was left open and Mr. Hubbard decided to go out for a walk. He had been in the Hollywood house only a day or two, and we were terrified when we figured out what had happened. When we realized he was gone, I went tearing out of the house to find him. Someone told me he had walked up toward La Brea Avenue, a very busy major street. I walked up and down La Brea and east and west of La Brea. I didn't know where he might be, but we had signs printed up, and Dorothy Jo and I posted them every place. And then it was night and he was gone—in Hollywood, a basset hound, old and deaf.

I got up early the next morning. Before I went to the studio, I looked up and down street after street. He was gone two days and two nights and part of another day. I went door to door. From talking to people, I figured out his route. He went south on La Brea, probably to Willoughby, and then east on Willoughby and realized he was not where he belonged. His instincts were right on, and he started north on Highland. At one time, he had traffic stopped in all four directions at the corner of Highland and Santa Monica.

I talked with people all along the route of my search. Mr. Hubbard's problem was that although he was a basset hound, he was not friendly to strangers. He ran from anyone who called him or tried to help him. I found people who did. They said he wouldn't come to them. He wouldn't get near them. As he came up Highland, he was hit by a car just south of Franklin but apparently not badly hurt. Even though he had been in the Hollywood house only two or three days, he was headed in the right direction. Then he went in a church at the corner of Franklin and Highland. I am sure he said a prayer.

A kind fellow who lived near the church put a bowl of milk on his front porch for Mr. Hubbard. The Good Samaritan told me that Mr. Hubbard wouldn't come up on his porch until he went back inside his house. Then Mr. Hubbard, who probably was ravenously hungry by this time, came up on the porch, quickly drank the bowl of milk, and headed north.

Heading north was a mistake. If Mr. Hubbard had gone only one more block west, and then made his turn north and gone just one block, he would have ended up right in front of his new Hollywood home. It's amazing what he almost accomplished.

As it was, Mr. Hubbard ended up five or six blocks up the hill above our home. I was able to stay on Mr. Hubbard's trail by literally going door to door and by talking with passersby on the street. Practically every moment that I wasn't taping

Truth or Consequences, I was searching for Mr. Hubbard. My mother or Dorothy Jo would go with me so we could cover both sides of the street from the car.

At this time, we were doing *Truth or Consequences* in the old Metromedia building on Sunset Boulevard. George Putnam was anchoring the news broadcasts for Channel 11 in the same building. I was so desperate by this time that I went to George and begged for his help. "George, I know this is an awful lot to ask, with everything going on in the way of news and everything you have to do, but I am trying to find my dog. If you would do something on the news about it, it might help me."

He said, "I'll be glad to do that."

I was astonished that he responded so quickly. I said, "Will you, really?"

"I will—really."

"George," I said, "you have no idea what this means to me."

He said, "Maybe I do." He asked me to come around his desk. I went around his desk, and under the desk, his dog was lying at his feet!

George Putnam went on the air that night and told the story of the missing Mr. Hubbard. He did that on the most watched broadcast, the *6:00 Evening News.* After searching again for several hours the next morning, I called in to Dorothy Jo from a pay phone. When she answered, she was very excited.

"There's a man up on the hill above us who thinks he has our dog!" I had thought I was on Mr. Hubbard's trail—and I was, but I was a day's travel behind him.

I talked with this gentleman on the telephone and I said, "Is he brown and white?"

"Yes."

"Does he have scars along his right back leg?"

"Yes, he does."

"That's my dog!"

My heart was pounding as I went rushing up that hill. Mr. Hubbard was on the front porch and this gentleman was sitting beside him. Mr. Hubbard was lying there, just completely worn out by his travels. The kind man was petting him and comforting him.

When Mr. Hubbard saw me his tail began thumping loudly on the porch.

Our hero had indeed seen the story of Mr. Hubbard on George Putnam's newscast, and within the hour, looked out his window and saw Mr. Hubbard sitting dejectedly in his driveway. Mr. Hubbard had apparently come to terms with the fact that he needed help and allowed this benefactor to take him in.

After profusely thanking the gentleman who saved Mr. Hubbard's life and trying unsuccessfully to give him a reward, I brought the tired, weary, hungry Mr. Hubbard home to a reunion with Dorothy Jo and Mother, complete with tears and lots of laughter. My only regret is that we didn't have a hidden camera. It would have been perfect for *Truth*.

Then I took him out in the yard. He was so hoarse that he could hardly make a sound. He had probably been barking at everything and everyone. He and I lay down in the grass to rest, but when he heard the dog next door barking, he dragged himself to his feet and made a sort of croaking sound as loudly as he could. He was back home and back in charge!

After Mr. Hubbard settled down for a rest, I called George Putnam. "You did it," I said. "This man had seen the story about my missing dog on the news. When you showed a picture of Mr. Hubbard, he knew that he had the right dog. I just called to thank you from the bottom of my heart."

He said, "No, you're not through yet. You've got to bring that dog down here and we're going to show the world what we did."

So I took Mr. Hubbard down, and we were on the *6:00 Evening News* again and we told our story. I had gotten Mr. Hubbard back after two days and two nights in Hollywood, in heavy traffic over blocks and blocks of strange streets—an old, deaf dog—all thanks to George Putnam, who loved animals, too.

. . .

Suerte (which means "luck" in Spanish) was a little beige mixed-breed dog that Dorothy Jo and I picked up one night in a restaurant parking lot. The attendant said, "She has been hanging around for several days. I give her water and something to eat from time to time." Dorothy Jo and I decided that she should be hanging around our house and being fed on time, every time. Hence, the name Suerte.

Juan, a completely charming little dog that my mother found on the street, was a mixed breed. He was so mixed that it was impossible to tell what and how many breeds he represented. He had large ears that came to a point, short legs, a long body, and a bushy tail. He was all black in color. One day I was sitting in the living room talking with Dick Woollen, director of programming for Metromedia at the time, when Juan came up to a window and looked in at us.

Dick asked, "What kind of dog is that?"

I said, "He's a Yugoslavian St. Azzi."

Dick said, "A *what*?"

I repeated, "He's a Yugoslavian St. Azzi. They are very rare in this country."

Dick said, "He looks like a mutt to me."

Mutt or Yugoslavian St. Azzi, Juan was a winner.

Enrique was a black Labrador mix, a sweet, gentle dog that captured your heart on sight. One of the nurses, Kathy Burns, who cared for my mother after her stroke found him in front of our house when she arrived for work. She brought him in, and he decided to stay. He never got on a bed unless my brother was visiting with us. Then he crawled up on Kent's bed and slept with him. Kent thought that was pretty neat.

• • •

I want to tell you about some of my more recent canine companions. Late one Friday afternoon, I got on the Hollywood Freeway and headed for Riverside to spend the weekend with my friend, Nancy Burnet. As usual on Friday, traffic was heavy and I did not arrive in Riverside until after dark. As I drove down a street beside a vacant lot, I saw the body of a dead dog that had been hit by a car. I continued on toward Nancy's house, but as I drove, I became concerned about the remote possibility that the dog I had seen might not be dead, but badly injured.

When I arrived at Nancy's home, I told her what I had seen and asked her to go back with me and check. When we reached the dog's body and got out of the car to check it out, we heard another dog growling from some shrubbery in the vacant lot. The dog in the street was indeed dead, and it was obvious that the dog growling at us from the shrubbery—a black long-haired terrier mix—was protecting the body.

You didn't have to be Sherlock Holmes to figure out that the two dogs were companions. One had been killed by an automobile, and the other was protecting his friend. Nancy and I were able to get the dog in the shrubbery to come out to us, but he wouldn't get in my car. He would not leave the body of his friend.

Nancy and I lifted the little body and carefully placed it on the backseat of my car, and promptly, the other dog jumped into my car to be beside his friend. It was such a beautiful display of love and loyalty that Nancy and I were both in tears.

The courageous little dog who so bravely protected the body of his friend was not wearing a collar. He had no identification of any kind. But his days of running the streets as a stray were over. I decided on the spot that he deserved the very best life that I could provide for him and that is exactly what he had for the rest of his life.

I named him Federico. He and I were in a picture together that was featured on a poster distributed all over the country during a national spay/neuter campaign sponsored, on my behalf, by CBS. That same picture of Federico and me became the most popular fan picture I had during my years on television. People didn't just write for a picture. They wrote and asked for "that picture of Federico and Bob."

• • •

I also had a wonderful huge black Labrador retriever named Winston. Winston was not only a huge dog, he was a huge character with a huge personality. He appeared on *The Price*

Is Right to celebrate my eightieth birthday, and he was a huge success there, too. Everything about Winston was big, including his appetite. He ate more like a horse than a dog. I named him Winston because when he folded his hind legs and sat with his front legs straight out in front of him, from the rear he looked very much like that famous photo of Winston Churchill taken from the back, as Churchill sat at his easel painting.

Nancy Burnet picked Winston up off the streets. She used the old dodge "Please keep him for a few days while I find him a home." Of course, the idea is that you will become so fond of the dog that you will keep him. I have used the trick myself—and frequently, it works. I laughed at Nancy for trying it on an old pro, but I took in Winston and was happier for it.

• • •

My house isn't all cats and dogs. I have rabbits, too—Mr. Rabbit and his Honey Bunny. Mercedes, my house manager—she's beyond housekeeper—found Mr. Rabbit one winter morning, shivering from the cold in a yard up the street. He was only a baby. When I couldn't find where he belonged, it became obvious that he belonged with me.

I had just bought a big-screen television set and two recliners for what was to become a television room. I decided that room could be a temporary home for my new friend, whom I named Mr. Rabbit. Before I could buy more furniture or decorate what was to have been a television room, Mr. Rabbit destroyed it. He tore up the recliners, chewed the wires in the television, and chewed holes in the carpet and the curtains. You might say that he redecorated the room more to his tastes. Knowing that I didn't really need a television room and that Mr. Rabbit was thoroughly enjoying himself, I just let him have at it. A man has to have his priorities.

I didn't want Mr. Rabbit to be lonely, so I went to a rescue group and found a little black female friend for him. It seemed logical since he is white. I adopted her and called her Honey Bunny. Folks warned me that the two rabbits might not get along well at first—they might require a period of adjustment. Not so. It was love at first sight!

Somehow Mr. Rabbit broke his leg a few months ago. During his rehabilitation, he had to be kept in a corral to restrict his movements. Honey Bunny insisted on staying in his corral with Mr. Rabbit and nursing him. She would come out of the corral and romp around occasionally, and then she'd go back to the gate and wait for it to be opened so she could get back on duty as Mr. Rabbit's nurse. Mr. Rabbit and his Honey Bunny are a darling couple.

My loyal house manager, Mercedes, adores Mr. Rabbit and his Honey Bunny. She does everything possible to assure that they are a healthy and happy couple. She is sure that they have every toy a rabbit might like, stools and a couch to jump up on—she even constructed a burrow for them. If you stepped into the room, you would assume some sort of disaster had occurred. Not so; it is a Mercedes-created rabbit heaven.

Dulce (which means "sweet" in Spanish) was a calico cat who came into the yard one day and meowed her way into my heart. Dulce was about ten years old when Mr. Rabbit came to live with us. Before I adopted Honey Bunny, Dulce would go into Mr. Rabbit's room and groom him or just hang out. Even if Mr. Rabbit became too obstreperous in his play, Dulce never scratched or bit him. Dulce would just lift a paw and gently push him away.

Winston liked to visit Mr. Rabbit's room, too. Mr. Rabbit would stand on his hind legs and examine Winston's large ears. It was always very congenial, but I made it a point to be right beside them any time Winston visited Mr. Rabbit.

. . .

For a short time, I didn't have a dog living with me, which was unusual. At that time, my brother Kent went out to an animal shelter in the Valley once a week and took pictures of dogs and put them on the Internet to try to help them get homes. He saw a sweet mix of golden retriever and chow named Jessie out there. She was fairly big and she was certainly no puppy, but he thought she was a wonderful dog and that she would be a good companion for me. He started selling Jessie to me that day. I told him I had several trips coming up and that I didn't want to get a dog at that point. He let it drop for a few days. Then he noted sadly, "You know, this dog hasn't been adopted and the shelter will have to euthanize her. They really have kept her longer than usual because she is such a great dog, but it's getting close."

Finally, a few days later he said, "The time has come, you're going to have to—"

I cut him off: "All right, bring Jessie to my house."

That night he showed up with Jessie, and she immediately checked out the yard, looked the house over, and made herself at home. Right from the beginning, she won the hearts of all my friends and visitors. She is very friendly with people, but other dogs were a different story. She was once more aggressive with other dogs than any dog I had ever had. The first time we took a walk she saw a dog half a block away and barked wildly. When she actually got near another dog, she reared on her hind feet like a stallion, pulling against the leash and pawing the air. It shocked me how really aggressive she was. The chow breed is very possessive, very protective. I suspect she thought these other dogs were going to attack me. She seemed to be trying to protect me. She had been trained to sit, and I took advantage of that. When another dog approached, I told her to sit and then forcibly restrained her. When the other dog went on its way, I said, "Good girl," and gave her a cookie. In a short time, Jessie was so much improved that I had to switch from cookies to tiny treats. Jessie was losing her girlish figure.

Jessie has trained me very well. Now I take a pocket full of treats with me on our walk. When we meet a dog and she behaves, she gets a treat. Occasionally, when she doesn't behave herself, she'll look up for the treat and I'll say, "No." She's bright enough to figure this all out.

Another story involving Jessie began like a scene out of a Lassie movie. I let Jessie out one morning and sat down to eat breakfast. In a matter of moments, Jessie burst back into the breakfast room. The expression on her face plainly said: "I have seen something most unusual. Please follow me and see for yourself."

I followed her out into the yard, but I was not very surprised to find two mallards, a male and a female, swimming slowly about in our pool. In past years, when they were migrating, ducks had landed in our pool to rest. I explained this to Jessie and assured her that the ducks would leave soon. I was wrong.

The ducks stayed, built a nest out of the way behind the pool, and the mother duck laid twelve eggs—that's right: an even dozen. For the next three months, Mercedes and I were busy, busy, busy.

I had a temporary fence installed to protect the mother duck and her babies from Jessie. The father duck had already taken a few bows and split. He did return three or four times during the three months, but apparently he was satisfied with what Mercedes and I were doing because he never hung around long.

Mercedes and I took a crash course in duck care and feeding. My pool man quit. I hired another pool man, and he quit, too. I hired a third pool man and he stuck it out. He'll be my pool man forever. Mornings and late afternoons, Mercedes laid out a veritable buffet for the duck family: corn mash, bread, chopped lettuce, the works.

I'll never forget the day Mercedes shouted, "Mr. Barker, Mr. Barker, come quick." There were all twelve baby ducks lined up on the edge of the pool. The mother duck was in the pool and you just knew she was quacking, "Come on down! The water's fine!" Gradually, one or two at a time, the babies jumped in and swam for the first time. It was an exhilarating moment for the duck family, for Mercedes, and certainly for me. I was also happy to see that the three little ramps we had installed on the edge of the pool allowed the ducklings to waddle safely up out of the pool and back into the nest.

That first swimming lesson was matched only by the thrill Mercedes and I felt when we saw the baby ducks fly a few feet above the water. Next, the baby ducks were able to take short flights—first in our yard and then around the neighborhood.

Finally, they were ready to move on with their lives. Just as they had first jumped in the pool, they flew away—one or two at a time. That wonderful mother duck stayed for two days to be sure all of her babies had made it; then she flew away, too.

Having the ducks visit was really a beautiful experience, one for which I am genuinely grateful. However, when the beautiful experience was concluded, I had the pool drained, thoroughly cleaned, and painted, and I installed a new pool filter.

What's Right About
The Price Is Right?

When I started doing the revised version, *The New Price Is Right,* in 1972, the show was an immediate smash success. Ratings were strong, attendance was robust, and the show's popularity gained momentum rapidly. Still, none of us could have predicted that the show would go on to be the longest-running game show in television history. Many of us involved in the show continued to work for *The Price Is Right* for decades and decades. That includes directors, producers, stagehands, cameramen, models, contestant coordinators, announcers, and, of course, me. That is a tribute not only to the success and longevity of the show, but also to the fun we all had. The reason many of us continued to do the show for such a long time was because we all loved it. When you do something you love for work, that is indeed a blessing. We took pride in keeping the show fresh and lively, and we took pride in the tremendous success of the show.

One of the reasons for the fast-moving and always changing nature of *Price* was the number of games we had in the rotation. We constantly developed new games. The audience loved the variety, and, of course, people picked out their favorite games and looked forward to seeing them on the program. The fundamental concept of all the games was always based on price, but we had so many variations and so many fun sound effects, lights, bells, and amazing props that it was a kaleidoscope of visual entertainment. Nevertheless, these games were carefully conceptualized, and we continued to brainstorm and experiment and try new things. Of course, we would play different games every day.

We were not only playing different games on *Price* each day, but within the same game, each contestant was different with a different personality and the prizes changed, and it made for an entirely different game. Let's say you play Ten Chances with one lady. The next time you play it, it is entirely different because now you have a male contestant or a teenager or another woman with a completely different personality. Who knows? And the game changes completely with the personality of the contestant.

I used to say when you watched *Truth or Consequences*, you never knew what was going to happen—because I was the host, and *I* never knew what was going to happen. I felt the same way about *The Price Is Right*. When I arrived at the show, they would hand me a list of the games we were going to play. I would look them over and I knew how we played them, but I had no idea what might happen with the contestants, and I would not know until I got a contestant onstage and saw his or her reaction and the audience's reaction to the contestant. At that moment, I would decide in which direction to go to get the most out of the game.

And you never knew who was going to correctly guess the prices. Some people knew them amazingly well, and other people had very little knowledge about them. But on the show, it did not make any difference. A ridiculous bid could be just as much fun as an accurate bid, so far as the crowd reaction was concerned. And you never knew who was going to win. Some people knew the games very well, and others looked panicked and confused—but even those confused folks could surprise you. I couldn't tell who was going to win. I have seen people walk off that show with hoards of money and prizes, and I would never have imagined them doing so well. That was the beauty of the show.

* * *

Eventually, we had about eighty different games in rotation on the show. I came up with several. Roger Dobkowitz developed the most games. Our director, Bart Eskander, was very creative. Anyone who worked for FremantleMedia could submit an idea for a game, and sometimes they worked. The inspiration for game ideas came from various sources. For example, Plinko was based on an old arcade pinball-like game called pachinko. Created by Frank Wayne, it had its debut in 1983. Plinko went on to become one of the audience's all-time favorite games on *The Price Is Right*.

Everyone has his or her favorite games. Cliff Hangers was a

big hit with audiences and contestants. People also loved the Clock Game. One of the games always associated with a huge prize was Golden Road. People would scream at the very mention of Golden Road. It gave the contestant a chance to win three prizes, and the third prize was always something in the category of a Viper. Naturally, that game elicited tons of excitement from audiences and contestants.

I didn't have a favorite game, but I particularly liked the games that gave me an opportunity to interact with the contestants a lot and, in so doing, to create excitement and laughter. Three Strikes, Triple Play, and It's in the Bag fit in that category.

In addition to the games, the prizes and the showcases were an important part of *Price*'s appeal to audiences. Cars were the most popular prize, and every year the cars got bigger, flashier, more glamorous, and more expensive. The first car I gave away on *The Price Is Right* was a Chevrolet Vega with a price tag of $2,650. As time went on, we had to remodel game props to accommodate five numerals instead of four because we couldn't get cars with a price of less than $10,000. At *Price,* we knew a thing or two about inflation.

But we still gave away new cars—sports cars, convertibles, and all kinds of expensive luxury cars that were unusual—and people went crazy over them. We gave away Lincoln Continentals, Cadillacs, and Chevrolets. We gave away that popular, expensive Dodge Viper. As I mentioned earlier, we had made the decision to give away only American-manufactured cars. This may have cost the show a little more, but we felt it was the right thing to do, to show support for the nation's industry and to help promote American cars. Some of the foreign car companies were offering cars at lower prices and offered us substantial discounts on cars, but we stuck to our guns and it all worked out. And there were plenty of beautiful American cars that were ecstatically received by our contestants.

As my animal rights activism and concerns became more intense, I was able to implement certain changes on *The Price Is Right*. By the early 1980s, the show was no longer giving away fur or leather products as prizes. We stopped giving away aquariums and fishing equipment. And for years I ended the show with: "Help control the pet population. Have your pets spayed or neutered." These were not critical changes or modifications to the show, but it was a by-product of my increased awareness and involvement with animal rights. Out of respect for my beliefs and my vegetarianism, the staff stopped putting meat on the grills and barbecues that we gave away. They would have vegetables sitting on the grill. It may sound like a minor thing, but it was a wonderful gesture, a subtle statement, and a sign of the consideration on the part of the staff.

• • •

The showcases were often elaborate set pieces, and our staff did a superb job putting these displays together. People look at *The Price Is Right* and think that the show is simple and relatively easy to produce, but there is a great deal of preparation (far more than most people imagine) in bringing everything together to produce the show. It is a fast-moving show, which makes it difficult for the cameramen and a challenge for the stagehands, who are constantly shuttling props, games, and prizes around the set. The cameramen and other technicians, announcer, and models rehearsed the presentation of the showcases and prizes. I didn't attend the rehearsals, but for the others, they were a crucial part of preparation. The logistics alone are a challenge when you are dealing with the elaborate games and the huge prizes. All of these things have to be assembled, moved, and stored.

Nevertheless, when *The Price Is Right* went on the air, it immediately resembled a party atmosphere, and the enthusiasm was infectious. The audience's energy fueled the contestants, the contestant's energy fueled the audience, and everyone, including the staff of the show and myself, could feed off the energy and reactions of the crowd. One of the best compliments I ever received as host of the show is related to this energy level. I made the games as exciting as I could. I tried to make *Price* a daily special event. A frequent comment, coming from different executives at the network or people in the industry, was that the energy level in our studio was the highest they had ever seen. They would say, "I watch this show, and you have been doing it for twenty-five years, and you come out there every day and make it look like the very first day of the show." That compliment meant I was earning my money.

That is what I worked for at *Truth or Consequences* and *The Price Is Right*. I figured if we were going to do it, I wanted to do it as well as I could do it that day, and I would often say that to the folks in the dressing room. We would be talking about something, and I would say, "All right, it is time to go. Let's go out there now, and let's do this just as though it were opening day!" And away we would go. You can do that when you are enjoying something. If you did not like the show and you did not want to be there, then you should find another job. I loved doing both *T or C* and *Price*. So did my colleagues. And it showed.

The party would start in the audience line outside the studio. People came from all over the country to attend the show. There were all races, all ages, all economic levels, and together they were having a party out there. They would be dancing, telling jokes, telling stories, and getting to know each other. On the show, everyone was cheering each other on. There was something inspiring and uplifting about that. Obviously, we were not solving the world's problems, but just seeing so many different kinds of people, everyday people, coming together in such a festive mood and rooting each other on was a tremendously encouraging sight.

Once the audience of 325 or so came into the studio, the party intensified. I wanted to maintain that energy and enthusiasm. One way I did that was to keep talking with the audience during commercials and stop-downs. I learned early on to keep the audience engaged and to keep the energy level up. On many shows, during a break, the host would step off and let the announcer take over. I never did that. I did not want to let the audience relax. I wanted to keep them ready to play the next game. I didn't want to let them get tired or distracted. I wanted to keep them up and with me, so that when we started the next game, they were all pumped and excited.

I have had people who have been in television for years tell me they had never seen anyone else do what I did: staying out there to roam around and talk with the audience during the breaks. I had fun myself, getting them to laugh, talking about anything and everything, fielding questions, getting to know them. Even little things would make an impact. I remember one time at the end of the show, we had the winner's friends come up onstage to celebrate his victory. One of the men had a baseball cap on, and he put it on my head. Immediately, I turned it around and wore it backwards. The audience had sympathy for an old man trying to regain his youth.

• • •

I have often said that the success of *The Price Is Right* was derived from the spontaneity involved with the audience and the contestants. That and the fast-moving nature of the show. People think game shows are easy. They are not. First of all, you have to have a strong basic premise for a game show to succeed. Some people think they can have a weak premise, but that with dancing girls and flashing lights, the show can succeed. It does not work. The television audience for a game show is more sophisticated than most people realize. If the show is not offering genuine entertainment, they are not going to watch it. Another sign of popularity is imitation, and international editions of *The Price Is Right* have been produced in twenty-eight countries. Representatives of some of these foreign productions spent a week or two with us, learning how we did things, before they tried to produce their own shows. *The Price Is Right* was among the highest-rated shows in England and Italy and has continued to be popular around the world.

• • •

When I first started doing *Truth or Consequences*, the Academy did not have Emmys for daytime television. Later on, I did *Truth or Consequences* in syndication, and the Academy did not have Emmys for syndicated programs. It was only once I began doing *The Price Is Right* that I became eligible to win an Emmy Award for daytime television. I received my first Emmy for the 1981–82 season, and it was just after my wife had passed away. I regret that I did not get at least one while she was with me because she had been such an important part of me getting any. Without her, I would never have received even one. After doing everything possible to help me, Dorothy Jo saw me get my first national show, *Truth or Consequences.* She was with me for *Price* and a long list of specials, too.

Speaking of the Emmys, I got to know Alex Trebek, the host of *Jeopardy!,* at the Emmys. I found him to be a very bright and fun fellow. I have always thought he did *Jeopardy!* exceedingly well. He is perfect casting, just right for that show. He impresses viewers as being erudite; he is pleasant and has a fine voice. I always thought he was a perfect choice for *Jeopardy!,* and he must have been because the show has been so successful.

When I retired, Alex wrote me a beautiful letter. He sent it to me about a month before my last show. He said in the letter, "As I approach my fiftieth year in our business, I am able to more fully appreciate the tremendous accomplishments of your half century. I congratulate you." It was a wonderful gesture on his part, and I was very touched. He also sent a generous check for the DJ&T Foundation. That meant a lot to me as well.

On the subject of other hosts, I have always admired Art Linkletter. When I was first starting out, working for KTTS radio station in Springfield, Missouri, Linkletter was doing *House Party* on CBS, and I used to hear his show every day when I worked my shift. When I heard his voice, the thing that came to my mind was a stream bounding down a mountain. In that wonderful voice, he would talk about his home, his family, and what they had been doing, and it brightened your day just to listen to him.

Years later, when he was a guest on *Truth or Consequences,* he told me backstage, "I've been watching you, kid. You're going to be around a long time." That thrilled me because I admired him immensely. He was an excellent guest on the show as well.

Groucho Marx was another host I admired. He was also a guest on *Truth,* and he said, "You know, when I watch you, I keep waiting for you to act like other game show hosts, but you never do." And I took that as a huge compliment because when he became a game show host, he did *You Bet Your Life.* He did not act like other game show hosts, either.

• • •

The Price Is Right juggernaut of success rolled on. We passed milestone after milestone. Millions of dollars in prize money handed out. We logged our 5,000th show (and actually logged 6,500 shows before I retired). We passed *Concentration* as the longest-running game show. In 2001, *TV Guide* called *The Price Is Right* the number one game show of all time. There were prime-time evening specials. There were anniversary shows. I was pleased that we were able to do shows dedicated to military servicemen and women. Those were very popular. We featured the different branches of the military, and we had audiences made up entirely of military personnel. It was our way of paying tribute to them, and we received bundles of letters thanking us. We also did shows honoring the police and fire department personnel who had been involved in rescue and recovery efforts after the Pentagon and World Trade Center attacks. These were also very special shows, and we all felt proud to be associated with them.

. . .

As each year passed, there were changes and differences that were evident in *Price,* but the fundamentals of our success remained the same. We had newer games, gadgets, and devices. We had more modern props and prizes. Filming, editing, and sound technologies improved, and we rolled out dozens of new games, but the show remained focused on the contestant and the concept was always based on prices. The audience dressed differently, wore their hair differently, and in general became much more casually attired. The first time I interviewed an attractive young lady and I realized that her tongue was pierced, I knew that time had passed me by.

I have said that the biggest change on *The Price Is Right* over the years was the color of my hair. They tinted my hair for years. When tinting began to cause my hair to be blue, they tried dyeing my hair instead, and after a period of time, dyeing gave my hair a red cast. Neither was attractive.

In 1987, I went on vacation and let my hair go gray, and when I came home everyone agreed that it looked better gray than tinted or dyed, so I decided that gray it would be. But we had taped ahead, so on Tuesday I had dark hair, and on Wednesday my hair was gray. I got a card from a man in the Midwest who wrote, "Bob, you must have had one hell of a night!"

It was a little revolutionary for the time. I do not think there was another gray-haired game show host on the air then, but I felt good about it, the audience felt good about it, and we marched on into the future. As I have said, people see me on television, and because I have never been anyone other than Bob Barker—I mean, never assumed another character—they feel that they know the real me. When I came out with my silver hair, it was no different. What they see is what they get. The viewers heartily approved.

• • •

While I did *Truth or Consequences* shows at remote locations, we always shot *The Price Is Right* at the CBS studio in Hollywood. *Price,* with all of its props and games and prizes, is not an easy show to travel, but we did try it one time. We decided to do a show in Las Vegas in 2002 at the Rio Hotel. The crowd that descended on the hotel in hopes of getting in to see the show was far larger than what the hotel had anticipated. It was estimated that ten thousand people filled the hotel and sidewalks for blocks around the hotel. Admittedly, crowd control was a problem, but that huge gathering was also an exciting testimonial to the popularity of *The Price Is Right.*

I was in bed when my phone rang about 4:00 a.m.—it was an executive at the hotel. He said, "We have a problem. We have ten thousand people here for your show."

"You don't have a problem," I said. "You have a problem when you have only a few people for a show. This is wonderful." And I went back to bed.

Later I was told that there were nearly one thousand people roaming around the hotel at four thirty in the morning, trying to get in line for tickets, and we were not shooting until evening. The crowd grew as the morning broke, and eventually police had to be called in to handle the crowds. In that sense, there was a problem. But the problem attracted media attention coast to coast. And that's good.

• • •

After Mark Goodson passed away, *Price* was sold to All American Television. Then All American Television sold the show to FremantleMedia. Syd Vinnedge was an executive with All American Television, and joined Fremantle at the time Fremantle purchased *Price*. Syd is now the executive producer of *The Price Is Right*. He is a good friend who has always been helpful to me professionally and personally, and I wish Syd much success with *The Price Is Right* for many years to come. He deserves it, and so do the folks who work with him on the show.

10

Hurray for Hollywood!
1950–1981

A few chapters back, I wrote that Dorothy Jo and I came to California by way of Palm Beach, Florida. Actually our sense of direction was not that bad. We had enjoyed Florida so much when I was in the navy that we decided to try it as civilians. I was twenty-five years old when I auditioned for a job at WWPG, a lovely little station on the beach in Palm Beach, and I was hired. The manager of the station, Charlie Davis, also helped Dorothy Jo get a job teaching biology at West Palm Beach High School.

We lived in Florida from the summer of 1949 to the summer of 1950. The highlight of the year for me professionally was my performance as Santa Claus during the Christmas season.

I claim, and the claim has never been disputed, that I was the best Santa Claus that Palm Beach ever had—or probably will ever have. Santa Claus was sponsored by a couple of tire stores in Palm Beach. He would appear at one store and then the other every other day—well, actually every other evening. You see, Santa was on the radio during the cocktail hour—a huge advantage when it came to ratings.

I speak of Santa Claus in the third person because when I stepped out of my Palm Beach sandals, slacks, and sport shirt and into my authentic-in-every-detail Santa suit, I became Santa. Even the chap who owned the tire stores said the transformation was phenomenal. He agreed that I became Santa. I shall always cherish the Santa experience. The awe and wonder in the eyes of some of the tots brought a lump to my throat, and I dealt with them with all the respect and tenderness that I could muster.

But there were the older kids, too. One kid, about nine years old going on nineteen, said, "What would you do if I reached up there and pulled that phony beard right off your face?"

Santa replied, "If you even touch Santa's beard, you might not live long enough to grow a beard yourself."

Being heard during the cocktail hour, Santa received bags of mail not only from children but from adults as well. One lovely lady wrote, "Dear Santa, my husband and I listen to you every evening. The more martinis we have, the more we love Santa." It was a merry Christmas, but Santa was canceled on December 26, so he and Mrs. Claus decided to go to California as soon as the school year ended.

• • •

While we were in Florida, Dorothy Jo and I did some modeling for Nelson Morris, a New York photographer who came down to Palm Beach to shoot photos for a gasoline company. Hers was the face that launched a thousand ships—presumably with cargoes of gasoline. I was a smiling gas station attendant. For years in Florida, our faces peeked out at you from ads on road maps.

During one of our photo sessions, I told Nelson that we were heading west, and he kindly suggested that I meet a colleague of his in Hollywood who might have some work for me as a model until I could land employment in radio. He gave me his colleague's card, for which I thanked him (more on that later).

Dorothy Jo and I arrived in Hollywood on August 13, 1950. I had no job, no agent, no contacts of any kind. We were candidates ripe for starving. I remember we were up on Los Feliz where it turns left and comes down to Franklin, on the eastern edge of Griffith Park. We looked out over the city, and it was a blanket of smog. Dorothy Jo turned to me and said, "Barker, what have you gotten me into?" But in a very short time, she came to love Hollywood, and she loved it until the day she died. How could we not love Hollywood? It has been so good to us.

Upon our arrival in the entertainment capital of the world, the first item on the agenda was an apartment, which Dorothy Jo promptly found on Las Palmas, just south of Hollywood Boulevard, and only two blocks from the offices of Ralph Edwards Productions, where I would sign a contract six years later.

It was a large two-story apartment house with Mediterranean-type architecture built around an attractive courtyard. We had a first-floor one-bedroom apartment with a dining area. The appliances were furnished and Dorothy Jo wasted no time buying furniture. Within a few days, Dorothy Jo, who loved to entertain, was ready to have a party. All we needed were guests, and it wasn't too long before we had those, too.

Our apartment was only a half block north of Sunset Boulevard, a short stroll for us to see the famous Hollywood Christmas parade in December of 1950. We thought it was very exciting to wave to the stars as they rode by. Dorothy Jo and I had the pleasure of riding in the Hollywood Christmas parade together several times during the ensuing years. In 2007, I was grand marshal of the Hollywood Christmas parade, and was joined in the grand marshal's antique limousine by my brother, Kent, and his lovely wife, Beth. My heart ached as I waved to the folks at the corner of Sunset and Las Palmas, where Dorothy Jo and I had stood and waved to the stars more than a half century ago.

Once we were ensconced in our Hollywood digs, I went to visit the photographer whose card I had been given back in Florida. His studio was a short drive from our apartment on Vine Street south of Sunset Boulevard. Unfortunately, he had no work for me, but he suggested that I go see a friend of his who might be able to use me. In fact, he picked up the phone and called his friend, who agreed to see me immediately. I drove down Vine to Santa Monica Boulevard, where the friend who might be able to use me was located. I was ushered right into this fellow's office by a woman of sixty or more who wore too much makeup.

His office was reasonably well furnished: dark wood, very masculine. The man was wearing a good-looking white shirt, a nice tie, and no coat. He had a good tan and his hair was carefully combed. I remember the whole scene vividly, because although it took him about ten minutes to say so in carefully couched language, the guy who might be able to use me offered me an opportunity to work in pornographic movies.

I laughed all the way home. I couldn't wait to tell Dorothy Jo. I rushed in and said, "Honey, I have been offered a role in a pornographic movie."

Dorothy Jo said, "Did you take it?"

. . .

In 1950, there was an FM radio station on Sunset Boulevard, not too far from our apartment, that was intended to become the mother station for an FM network. I decided to try to get a job as a salesman at this FM station. I wanted to sell some sort of audience participation show and host it myself. I made an appointment with the sales manager, a Scot named Worthy Murchison, who was destined to become a good and very amusing friend. Worthy and I talked for ten or fifteen minutes, which was all it took for him to determine that I had never sold anything, but our conversation had been fun. Worthy had a dry sense of humor that I thoroughly appreciated, and although I was in his offices under false pretenses, he seemed to enjoy our conversation, too.

He said, "I am about to go out to the Cracker Barrel Market in the San Fernando Valley and pitch a show to originate in the market. You go with me and help me sell it. If we do, you can host it."

I said, "Let's go!"

We went, and we struck out. But in addition to being sales manager of a radio station, Worthy managed an apartment house, and on the way back to Hollywood, we stopped at an appliance store for something Worthy needed for the apartment house. It was Rick's Appliances on Ledge, east of Lankershim Boulevard in North Hollywood.

Roy Rick was a big, broad-shouldered, good-looking guy who had hitchhiked out to Los Angeles from Iowa with only eight dollars in his pocket. He had a series of jobs and ended up cutting meat in a supermarket, where he had a chance to meet lots of housewives. Perhaps it's better said that lots of housewives had a chance to meet Rick. Rick (people seldom called him Roy) decided that he should take advantage of his popularity in that part of the San Fernando Valley, and he decided that an appliance store in North Hollywood would be a good way to do it.

That's the store Worthy and I walked into in August of 1950. Worthy, Rick, and I talked long enough for Rick to learn that I had just arrived in Hollywood and was seeking employment as the host of an audience participation radio show. Suddenly Rick said, "Bob, I like the cut of your jib. I want you to do a show for me."

As I was wondering what a jib was, Rick went on to say the auditorium of the Department of Water and Power office on nearby Lankershim Boulevard was available to him free of charge. Rick said that the water and power company would provide a home economist and all supplies required for a cooking class. They would also provide a freezer demonstration, a washer and dryer demonstration, or a demonstration of any other appliance—so long as it plugged in.

All of this would be free, Rick said, if we could fill the auditorium with women who could be considered prospective purchasers of appliances powered by electricity.

"What do you think, Bob?" Rick asked.

I said, "That's great, but what about the cost of radio time and my salary?"

"I'm a Hotpoint appliance dealer and a Zenith television dealer, and I sell lots of both. They'll split the tab if you can bring in the women."

"I'll bring them if I have to drive by and pick them up," I said. And I did.

I should say we did. Dorothy Jo and I sat down that night and put together some ideas that were time-tested winners in Missouri and/or Florida, and I was back at Rick's Appliances the next day. Rick had the show sold to Hotpoint and Zenith before I got home—well, almost. The deal was signed, sealed, and delivered very quickly. Worthy Murchison was a part of it, in that he represented the radio station KWIK in Burbank and we bought the time from him. Worthy was a busy young man: KWIK, an FM radio network, and an apartment house. When did he sleep?

Dorothy Jo and I had arrived in Hollywood in August, and we did our first show for Rick in September. The show was very successful. Women were coming from the far corners of the San Fernando Valley to attend. Rick was seeing lots of new faces in his store, too. We were all happy.

But the best was yet to come. The folks with Bekins Furniture sales division heard about the show and paid us a visit. As a result, I did a few television commercials for them. It was my first appearance on television, and Dorothy Jo and I didn't even own a television as yet. The show was a unique method of selling appliances, and it wasn't long before all the manufacturers were sending representatives out to North Hollywood to scout the action.

One of these scouts was Hal Klapper, a young executive with Westinghouse. Westinghouse had a talent show on the local NBC television station called *Your Big Moment*. Some of the people with Westinghouse weren't happy with the emcee, and Hal convinced them that I was the man they needed. *Your Big Moment* was my first television show as the host. I remember my opening was: "Welcome to *Your Big Moment,* the show that gives you—if you have the talent—your big moment on television." We had some really talented people—and a few who were not—on the show. Hal Klapper and his wife and Dorothy Jo and I became close friends, too.

Incidentally, the Department of Water and Power Building where I emceed my first show in California is only three blocks from where the Academy of Television Arts and Sciences complex now stands. In 2004, I was inducted into the Television Hall of Fame right there in the academy theater, and my bust is mounted on a pedestal in the academy courtyard. Dorothy Jo and I made the right decision when we aimed our yellow Studebaker west.

• • •

I was excited and very pleased to learn that Morris Tallon, an executive of the Southern California Edison Company, was in the audience for our show one day. Better still, I stole a glance at him from time to time, and he was laughing and applauding. I figured that had to be a good sign, and I was right. A couple of

Top: Giving cookies to Lupe, Carlos, and Juan. Above, left: Mr. Rabbit and Honey Bunny playing in the hallway. Above, right: Mama and baby ducks in the pool. Right: Jessie.

Above: With some of my Emmys. Opposite, top: Receiving a Lifetime Achievement Award at the Emmys. Opposite, bottom: The plaque commemorating the 5,000th show and naming Studio 33 the Bob Barker Studio.

Right: With a happy winner on *The Price Is Right*. Below: A special *Price Is Right* for the army.

Top: Dorothy Jo with the yellow Studebaker in front of our duplex in Lake Worth, Florida, 1950.
Left, and above: The ads Dorothy Jo and I modeled for in Florida for Kool-motor Motor Oil.

Above, left: Dorothy Jo and me, Christmas 1965, at a friend's house. Above, right: With Dorothy Jo on the stairs of our home. Below: Getting my star on the Walk of Fame, May 5, 1976. My mother is on the far left, Dorothy Jo and Ralph Edwards are beside me.

Above: Dorothy Jo and me. Left: Running on the beach in Biloxi during the 1980 Miss USA pageant.

Above: Hosting the Miss USA pageant.
Right: With past winners of Miss USA
and Miss Universe. Below: Nancy Burnet
and me leading an antifur march down
Fifth Avenue in New York City, 1990.

Left: Adam Sandler and me on location shooting *Happy Gilmore*. Below: Adam Sandler and me arriving in a golf cart for the premiere of *Happy Gilmore*.

Above: Taping the special celebrating my fifty years on television in 2007, with announcer Rich Fields and Barker's Beauties. Below: Dennis Weaver, Dinah Shore, and me on *The Dinah Shore Show*.

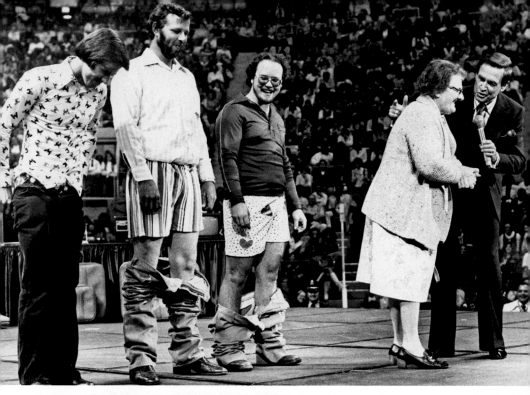

Top: Hosting *The Bob Barker Fun and Games Show* in St. Louis the night we broke the attendance record at the Old Checkerboard Dome. Above: Jackie Chan holds the bag for me, around 1975, just after he arrived in the United States. Left: With Roy Rogers and Dale Evans, grand marshals of the Rose Parade.

Above: With actress and my co-host June Lockhart interviewing the 1970 Rose Parade grand marshals: *Apollo 12* astronauts Charles Conrad Jr., Richard F. Gordon, and Alan L. Bean. Right: Interviewing parade grand marshal Lee Iacocca. Below: Loretta Swit, Zsa Zsa Gabor, and me at an antivivisection press conference.

Above: With Nancy Burnet.

PERFORMING ANIMAL WELFARE SOCIETY
AWARD OF OUTSTANDING ACHIEVEMENT
CELEBRITY
BOB BARKER
FEBRUARY 1988

Opposite: Holding an award from PAWS for my efforts on behalf of the *Project X* chimpanzees. Top: Testifying in Washington before a subcommittee of the Department of Agriculture regarding the treatment of captive elephants. Above: My house.

Above: Ed Stewart, Nancy Burnet, me, and Pat Derby at the PAWS Wildlife Sanctuary near San Andreas, California, May 2008. Below: With my family at home: Bob Valandra, Peter Kelly, Julie Valandra holding her son Noah, me, Hannah Valandra, Kent Valandra, Vicky Valandra-Kelly, and Kent Valandra Jr.

days later, I met with Mr. Tallon in his office in downtown Los Angeles. He was not a man to waste time with small talk. He promptly said, "Bob, you are doing one show a week out there in North Hollywood. How would you like to do six shows a week for Edison, all over Southern California?"

"I would like that," I replied.

And with those words, we launched a relationship of almost eight years for Dorothy Jo and me with the Southern California Edison Company. We did two shows a day, three days a week, in towns and cities from the beach to San Bernardino in the east, and from South Los Angeles to Lancaster in the north. Talk about experience—I got it, hours and hours of it. And no matter how much talent you have for doing audience participation, there is no substitute for experience.

Our shows for Roy Rick in the Department of Water and Power auditorium and in the Southern California Edison Electric Living Centers were immensely successful because they were unique in character. To the best of my knowledge, no utility had ever used a radio show to attract women to an appliance demonstration, and an audience participation show was the perfect vehicle.

To open the festivities, Dorothy Jo went out onstage, introduced herself, and expertly established a party atmosphere that prevailed throughout the day. An Edison home economist conducted an appliance demonstration that was informative and fun, and then out I came to select contestants to start the radio show. I chose some contestants before we began taping, but not all. I wanted folks in the audience to know they still had a chance to participate right up until sign-off.

One of the staples of our radio show was a contest in which

half a dozen ladies discussed such subjects as "my huband's worst fault," "my own worst mistake," "how to get a man," et cetera. Of course, the audience would choose the winner. Sometimes Dorothy Jo wrote a commercial to the tune of a well-known song, and I would have fun auditioning ladies by having them sing the scales. Eventually I chose a quartet and they sang our commercial.

Maybe I would go on a search for the lady who had been married the longest, the oldest lady, or the lady with the most children. The most middle-aged lady was sure to shock the winner. At that time, the average age of a woman in the United States was seventy-two, so you were middle-aged at thirty-six. Some women couldn't handle that.

One time I was looking for women who collected things and an elderly lady raised her hand.

"Madam, what do you collect?" I asked.

She said, "Sonny, I've been married four times, and it was quite a collection!"

How could a show with that kind of material possibly miss?

. . .

Although things were progressing splendidly, there was an uncertainty lurking in the background of all of our radio activity. I was still in the naval reserve, and the Korean War had broken out by this time. There was some speculation (actually, I considered it a strong possibility) that I would be called up for duty. All naval aviators were automatically in the naval reserve for a number of years. I was checked out in the Corsair, a propeller-driven plane, and they were using it at that time in Korea. I remember thinking that the navy might call me up to get more training in the newer jets, or they might want me to come and fly Corsair missions. Either way, I considered it a distinct possibility, and I remember thinking that if I did go back into the service, I might just stay in the navy because I did not feel like coming back out to Hollywood and starting all over again. But apparently my destiny was sealed because once again the war ended without my help, and I never piloted another airplane in my life.

Dorothy Jo and I also developed and sold our own local television show during this period. This show was on KHJ on Vine Street. I met Jerry Mertens, who was with an advertising agency, and Jerry had a client, an independent druggist who was not fond of the large drug chains. This client had a product he wanted to market and promote. He believed he had the solution to teenagers' complexion problems. The product was called Teen Tone. He wanted a television show that would attract teenagers, who would hopefully buy jars and jars of Teen Tone.

Dorothy Jo and I created a talent show and we focused on high school students. We called it *Talent in High*. We took talent from all the high schools in the area. Believe me, there were some talented young people available. We had singers and dancers and musicians of all kinds, and the show was very successful. Nevertheless, *Talent in High* ended after thirteen weeks. It was not because people did not like the show. The problem was marketing the product Teen Tone. There was no place to buy it because the creator refused to do business with drug chains. He insisted on selling it to independent drugstores, so it was almost impossible to find Teen Tone even if you wanted to buy it. I think I still have a jar or two. Maybe I should try eBay.

. . .

As I look back on this time, I recall how happy Dorothy Jo and I were. We were making friends and exploring Southern California, and it was an exciting time in radio and television. Hollywood, as always, was the epicenter of the action. The country was also still in the throes of post–World War II jubilant spirits and solid economic prosperity, and nowhere was that more evident than in Southern California.

One time shortly after we arrived in Hollywood, we were invited to a party on Hollywood Boulevard in an apartment not far from Hollywood and Vine. We were delighted to receive an invitation to a bona fide Hollywood party, one that was not far from us. It was one of those classic grand old apartment buildings built around a courtyard. It was a nice old apartment, and it was a big party. There were a lot of people there of every description, and the party got loud, and then louder, and then still louder. The apartment manager came out and complained about the noise, but the complaint was ignored. In fact, the party got even more raucous, and the manager called the police. The manager came and told the fellow who lived in the apartment, the host, that he had called the police, but the manager added, "You go ahead and make as much noise as you want. Have as big a party as you want because tomorrow you are gone. You are out of here."

Then the police arrived. Dorothy Jo and I did not want to discuss the party with the police if we could avoid it, and neither did a lot of other people. They started disappearing in all directions. Dorothy Jo and I chose to step out onto a fire escape, and it just so happens that we were joined out there by a midget. He was a very nice fellow and funny, and we enjoyed talking with him while we waited for the police to leave. I remember Dorothy Jo and I looked at each other, and it occurred to me that we really were a part of the Hollywood scene now—we were at a party on Hollywood Boulevard, hiding from the police with a midget on a fire escape.

Our life became even more Hollywood only a few years later. Dorothy Jo and I were living on Laurel Avenue in an apartment just above Sunset Boulevard when I signed to do *Truth*. I had received the call from Ralph, but I had not started the show yet. It was December 1956. I walked down to the cleaners near our apartment. I used to talk to the lady who managed the place. I said, "I have some news for you. I am going to host *Truth or Consequences*." It was already a famous show that had been on for years on radio and television. I told her that it was coming back, and I was going to host it. "This will be my first national show," I told her with pride.

And this lady looked at me and said, "Yes, now it is all up to you. You got your break. Now it is all up to you."

And I thought, "You know, she is right. It is all up to me," but I knew that I had Dorothy Jo in my corner. She was always there for me until October 19, 1981.

Earlier that year, we learned that Dorothy Jo was terminally ill with inoperable lung cancer, and we had a lot of talks. One time she said, "Do not be afraid of being alone. You will find great comfort and tranquility in solitude." And she was absolutely right. I have found great comfort and happiness alone.

I miss her tremendously, but I have found some peace in solitude. I enjoy being alone and reading or being with my dog and rabbits or writing or working in my office or whatever. She created a home for me, a home of comfort and security, with our animals and the things we loved in life, and I still live in that home. I have a routine in which I take great comfort.

Dorothy Jo passed away on October 19, 1981. Interesting thing—Dorothy Jo was born on February 25, 1924. My mother died on February 26. My mother's birthday was October 18, and Dorothy Jo died on October 19. We had been together since 1939, when we were fifteen years old. She really was the light of my life, and I have never thought about marrying again. She was responsible in so many ways for any success I may have had, and we were inseparable from the time we met. I have had many blessings in my life, but she was the greatest of them all.

11

The Beauty Pageants
and the "Fur Flap"

There was a tremendous amount of overheated publicity surrounding my departure from the Miss USA and Miss Universe beauty pageants, but I consider my twenty-one-year association with the pageants to have been an extremely positive relationship, and hosting those events was definitely something I enjoyed immensely. In the end, because of the clash between the fur coats and my passion for animal rights, it was impossible for me to continue with the shows. However, I would not want that to cast a shadow over the many years of fun and success we all had working on those pageants.

. . .

Both pageants were broadcast from Miami Beach for the first ten years, but later on we had invitations from cities all over the United States for Miss USA and from all over the world for Miss Universe. We went to El Salvador, Singapore, Australia, Puerto Rico, Hong Kong, Mexico, and other countries with Miss Universe, and we did Miss USA in New York, Buffalo, Miami, Biloxi, and other cities in the continental United States, as well as Puerto Rico.

Unfortunately, Dorothy Jo and I did not always have an opportunity to explore all of these fascinating places. John Christ and I (I'll tell you more about John later) were frequently tied up with details of the pageants, and I was still doing *The Price Is Right*—and for a while, *Truth or Consequences* as well. Sometimes we just had to fly in and fly out after the show, but other times we were able to explore some memorable locations.

I'll never forget the 1973 Miss Universe show we did in Greece at the majestic Odeon of Herodes Atticus, which stands at the foot of the Acropolis of Athens. It was a thrill to be there in the midst of all that history—the theater goes back to the days of Socrates. The show was live, like all of them, and in the evening under the stars. Many people thought it was the most beautiful show we ever did. They may be right. I'll never forget it.

The Miss Universe pageants were, as you can imagine, truly international events. We had interpreters giving stage directions in several languages. We had to search high and low for people who could translate questions and answers for the contestants from all over the world. The language barriers were always challenges in producing the shows from these exotic locations.

There were other challenges as well. In 1972, we were doing the Miss USA pageant down in Puerto Rico. About thirty miles from San Juan, at the Hotel Cerromar near the town of Dorado, we were headquartered in this big vacation hotel with lovely facilities, a couple of pools, and a gorgeous golf course. There were many tourists vacationing at the hotel. However, there was also a group of anti-Americans protesting daily outside the hotel. They shouted, "Gringo, go home," and other unprintable angry comments.

The night of the pageant, I was hosting the show live again, and we're rolling along. I have forgotten exactly what part of the show I was in, but there was a huge explosion. The stage rocked and the audience was obviously disturbed, but I just ignored it and kept moving through the show. I didn't know what the explosion was and naturally I was curious, but I finished the segment. When we went into the commercial break, Charlie Andrews, the producer of the show, didn't want me to be upset, so he said, "Don't worry about the explosion. It was just a refrigerator that blew up in the kitchen." Just then, another explosion rocked the stage.

I could not resist commenting, "Charlie, we're going to have to go out to eat because there goes the freezer."

The group of protesters had set off two bombs. The first bomb exploded in the parking lot near our control truck, which was the technical and directorial center for the show. Like the booth in a studio, it was in the truck that our director and top technicians were making decisions essential to the production of the show.

Obviously, the anti-American group knew the importance of the truck, and they were attempting to knock the show off the air by blowing it up—and possibly the director and the technicians with it!

The second bomb was set off on the fifth floor of the Hotel Cerromar, and it destroyed three rooms. It blew furniture off a balcony hundreds of feet toward the beach. The explosion itself or the flying debris could easily have killed someone. It was a miracle that not one person was hurt by either explosion.

A few months later, we had to return to the Cerromar hotel in Dorado to broadcast the Miss Universe pageant. Despite the fact that we had contracted with the government of Puerto Rico, many friends—and all of our wives—were telling us to forget it. No show was worth it. But we decided to risk it under carefully controlled circumstances. This time, security was everywhere. I remember flying into the San Juan airport, and a small plane took me from San Juan out to the hotel. I felt as though I were in the middle of a World War II movie. There were spotlights from the ground on the airplane, lights all around the hotel, and armed guards everywhere. There were no tourists at all in the hotel—only hotel employees and people involved with the pageant. They had plainclothesmen on every floor, and uniformed sentries surrounded the hotel. The government of Puerto Rico wanted to make sure we weren't blown up on their watch.

We were stuck in the hotel for six days. We went to dinner in the same dining room every night, and the contestants and folks working on the pageant were the only ones there. The hotel put on a floor show every night to entertain us—a flamenco dancer. We watched that same guy every night. If I never see another flamenco dancer again, it will be too soon. After dinner and the dancer, we were all bored. Everyone, including me, gambled every night—one of my few experiences with gambling (yes, I lost money). Anyway, thanks to the security, nothing happened. We did the show, and we all got out of there safely.

No matter where we were located, the pageant shows were always broadcast live. I was impressed by the ability of the young women who were pageant contestants to handle the pressure of live television. They were, for the most part, calm and collected, and it was a pleasure to work with such enthusiastic young ladies. There is a misconception that the young ladies in these pageants are not particularly intelligent. My experience over the course of twenty years is completely contrary to that notion. Obviously, in any group of young people, you're going to have some who are brighter than others, but all in all, the contestants were extremely sharp and savvy, in addition to being talented and attractive. By the time they have reached the level of Miss USA or Miss Universe, they had to have won several other pageants, and they had learned quite a bit. Most people would be surprised at the level of poise and maturity these young women possessed.

• • •

Despite all of the happy memories, I eventually left the pageants because of what came to be known as the "fur flap." On the one hand, it was kind of sudden and unexpected, but in retrospect, it was also a natural conclusion to the series of events that led up to it.

My passion for animal rights was a process of growing awareness for me. I wasn't always so aware or involved. I will be the first to admit it: In the 1960s, I gave Dorothy Jo a couple of furs as presents. She stopped wearing them and she stopped wearing leather jackets. Without criticizing me or anyone else, she quietly influenced me by example.

After doing some promotional work for the Society for the Prevention of Cruelty to Animals, Los Angeles (SPCALA), in 1979 I was asked to be honorary chairman of Be Kind to Animals Week in Los Angeles. I accepted, and as a result, I did interviews on radio and television and with newspapers. This led to invitations from animal-oriented groups to participate in their activities. I had contributed financially to animal organizations prior to that, but I had never become involved in their work. I decided to give it a try, and as I did, I began for the first time to really become aware of the terrible exploitation, cruelty, and mistreatment animals suffer in our country—or in the world, for that matter.

As my awareness grew, I began making changes in my life. Dorothy Jo suggested I become a vegetarian in 1980. I learned about the terrible things that happen in slaughterhouses, and I decided to cut out red meat. Then later I learned more about fishing and the treatment of poultry, and I stopped eating chicken and fish. Originally, I did it out of concern for animals, but I can also see why people become vegetarians for health reasons. My energy level rose sharply, and my weight has never been an issue. I felt better immediately. I do not think I ever would have been able to work as long as I did had I not become a vegetarian.

So for about seven years prior to the fur flap, which came during the Miss USA pageant of 1987, I had been increasingly active and outspoken on animal rights issues. As I learned more about the horrendous exploitation of animals, I felt compelled to do what I could to change the situation.

Looking back, I can see a progression of events leading up to the pageant controversy. I was fired from two radio shows for speaking out against laboratory research on animals. In the early 1980s, I convinced the producers of *The Price Is Right* to stop giving furs away as prizes. I had also resigned as host of the American Humane Association's Patsy Awards show, which honors animal actors and their trainers, when I learned that some trainers beat animals unmercifully to make them perform.

Animal exploitation comes in many forms, and the more I learned, the more appalled I was by the practices of the fur industry and the idea of slaughtering millions of animals for leisure coats, which are worn strictly to show off wealth. Wearing furs is a reprehensible method of displaying affluence. I've always said there are better ways. Diamonds, wristwatches, and automobiles are a few examples. There is no way to make a fur coat without causing pain to God's creatures. If you really want to impress people with how much money you have, buy a cloth coat and hang bills on it. The more money you have, the bigger bills you should use.

It was not just the killing of the animals to make a leisure garment, but it was the cruelty and methodology involved. First, there are the steel leg traps. The animals have their legs shattered in these traps; their bones are broken, their tendons and ligaments are crushed, and then they die a slow agonizing death. A trapped animal often suffers for days before death.

I remember hearing about many barbaric practices and atrocities, but I specifically remember one horrible instance where an Alaskan lynx was stuck in a leg-hold trap for six weeks until the trapper checked his traps. The lynx was able to stay alive so long only because another lynx in his family brought the poor creature food.

On farms and ranches all over the world—including the United States—animals are kept in cramped cages and subjected to drowning, neck wringing, poison gas, injection, and electrocution. I try to focus attention on these barbaric practices whenever I can. I have said that the fur industry is one of the worst exploiters of animals, whether they are trapping animals in the wild or raising them on farms.

* * *

Despite my growing enlightenment, I had really never encountered a conflict with my personal beliefs during my hosting duties. By 1987, I had been doing the beauty pageants for twenty years, and I always looked forward to doing them. They had become a very pleasant part of my life—and of my income. I didn't know it then, but my passion for animal protection was on a collision course with one of my favorite events, and something was going to have to give.

The dramatic confrontation occurred in 1987, in Albuquerque, New Mexico, site of the Miss USA beauty pageant. The pageant producers had awarded fur coats as prizes for years. Fur coats were standard fare at all of the pageants. After working on them for a couple of years, however, I was able to persuade the producers of the Miss Universe and Miss USA pageants to cease and desist. In 1987, I went to Albuquerque, New Mexico, to host the Miss USA pageant, knowing that a fur coat would be presented to the winner, but I also knew that fur coats would be a thing of the past, as of 1988. I arrived in

Albuquerque on Friday the thirteenth. The show was going to be broadcast on Tuesday the seventeenth.

On the first day, I was appalled to learn that in the swimsuit competition, the semifinalist contestants would be coming onto the stage wearing fur coats over their swimsuits. The swimsuit competition was to be on a winter wonderland type of set that resembled a northern New Mexico ski lodge. The women were going to stroll on the stage, wearing the fur coats, and then drop them and model in their swimsuits for the judges.

I didn't want to engage in a conversation right there on the spot on the rehearsal stage with a crowd of people watching, but I was immediately troubled. That night in my hotel room, I spoke on the phone with my close friend and animal activist associate Nancy Burnet. We both agreed I couldn't do the show if real furs were going to be worn and displayed by the contestants.

The pageant had put me in a position that would be untenable after speaking at various locations around the country urging people not to wear furs. It would have been hypocritical of me to appear if the furs were used, and it would have destroyed my credibility within the animal rights movement. I couldn't let down all of the people who had written me to lend their support for the cause.

For me, the decision was simple. For the producers of the show, it was more complicated. George Honchar, the producer of the pageant, was a friend of mine, and we had thoroughly enjoyed working together on the show. He was in a difficult position because, as he told me and the news media, the furs were part of a contract the pageant had with a New York furrier. He said the coats were a necessary part of the show because of the advertising commitments and that he depended on my professionalism not to break my contract.

I wasn't combative, but I was firm. I told them, "If the contestants wear fur coats, I can't participate."

The stage for a battle of wills was set. We met for an hour and a half on Monday night. George listened to me. I listened to him. Nothing was solved. I pleaded with him to arrange for fake furs to be used. He fell back on his obligations to his sponsors. George had a backup emcee ready in the wings to fill in for me. His name was Michael Young. He had been the emcee of the Miss Teen USA pageant.

Fortunately, our conversations leaked to the media. The story of our standoff became national news. It was labeled the "fur flap" by reporters and editors around the country. The fur flap was on the front pages of newspapers, on the radio, and on national television. People were reading and hearing about this guy who was willing to give up his job out of concern for the animals that suffered horribly in the production of fur coats. All of this national publicity was the best thing that ever happened to the antifur campaign.

The media was having a field day with this standoff, and I remember thinking that there had never been more media attention focused on the animal rights movement than during those few days. I learned later that CBS had received 568 telephone calls supporting me and my position, while eight calls (all from furriers) were received opposed to my position.

To his credit, George Honchar was scrambling to come up with a solution. One of the things I remember him saying during the dispute was "I'm not looking at throwing Bob's number of years with this event out the window."

I also remember that many of the contestants sympathized and respected my position on the fur coats. They were careful not to offend the pageant, but many of them were animal lovers and said that they supported my stand.

Finally, at the last hour, George Honchar arranged to use fantastic fake furs, though it took quite a bit of last-minute hustling to get them from an Albuquerque department store. We agreed that the women would wear fake mink and ermine furs in the ski lodge number, and I would fulfill my hosting duties. I would also announce as the women strolled by, "All of the ladies are wearing simulated furs."

I was tremendously happy. I told George that animal rights groups across the country would hail him as a hero. He said that he had made the switch because he had no doubt that I was going to stick to my position, and he was right.

When asked by the press how he would handle the furriers, George said, "I'll deal with them later." He also said to me, "This would have been a hell of a way to end our association."

I agreed that it would have been a terrible way to end our relationship. Sadly, my long, happy, and financially rewarding relationship with the pageants did indeed end the next year. As I noted, the pageant producers had agreed to no more furs in 1988, but they changed their minds.

I was surprised when I learned that they were going to continue to give away a fur coat. I pleaded with George Honchar once again: "Please don't put me in that position."

"It's just a twelve-second plug at the end of the show, and you don't even have to do it, a cohost will," he said.

But there was no budging in either of us that year. I promptly resigned as host. By quitting, I was fulfilling a pledge I had made in the previous year's controversy. In truth, it was all sort of anticlimactic compared to the year before. There was no last-minute standoff. There was none of the drama of the year before, though my resignation did gain quite a bit of media attention. "Fur Flap II," it was called, and again it was a boon to the antifur campaign.

It was simply the culmination of my increased awareness and sensitivity to animal rights issues. I wasn't bitter. I had done the pageant for twenty-one years. Certainly there was some sadness, but it was a matter of principle for me and a matter of business for the pageant. The Miss USA officials said that they respected my moral commitment, but theirs was a business decision. They had a long relationship with certain sponsors and advertisers, and they didn't want to change that.

My mother couldn't believe it. She was baffled that the pageant would rather lose me as a host than drop fur coats as a prize. Dear old mom. I'm glad that I helped raise awareness of animal cruelty in the production of fur products, and I'm glad that fur fashion has declined significantly in this country and around the world.

Of course, I continued to be active and vocal about animal rights issues long after those beauty pageant days. But I think that those two years were crucial moments in terms of raising public awareness. I realized that resigning from the pageants would be a sacrifice, but I really had no choice. The financial loss in no way compares to the importance of the issue with me.

The year I resigned, I was asked by protest groups to picket outside the pageant, but I did not want to do that. What concerned me was the possibility that I would be perceived as vindictive—involved in a feud with the officials of the pageant, which simply was not true. I did not want something I saw as a positive to come off as a negative.

. . .

In November of 1988, I led the first of two protest marches down Fifth Avenue in New York of about two thousand animal rights activists. Nancy Burnet, of United Activists for Animal Rights, marched right there beside me. The marches were held on Fur Free Friday, the Friday after Thanksgiving, which is the traditional kickoff day for holiday shopping. (Now they are held on Fridays near the Thanksgiving holiday.)

These marches and protests took place all across the country, from New York to Beverly Hills, and were huge in drawing attention to fur boycotts. Our rallies were successful beyond our wildest expectations. The nationwide protests got tremendous media attention.

The rallies I attended were organized by Trans-Species Unlimited, and its director Steve Siegel called me "the most vocal spokesman for the antifur movement in the world." Steve may have exaggerated a bit, but I liked it. There were signs that read "Shame," "Vanity," "Fur Is Murder," and "If You Don't Buy Them, They Won't Kill Them."

The protesters picketed in front of department stores and heckled customers wearing fur coats. There were some heated exchanges. By 1989, there were rallies and protests in over ninety cities across the country on Fur Free Friday. There were coffins filled with furs, there were coats splashed with red paint to symbolize blood, and there were demonstrations in front of department stores from Boston to Denver and from New

York and Pennsylvania to Orange County, California. People wore simulated leg traps. The people behind this cause were and are a very passionate group. They carried tape recorders broadcasting the cries of wounded animals. In Europe, I recall, activists spit on people who wore fur coats. It was a turning point, no question.

Over 120 different animal rights groups participated in the marches around the country, and while we focused on fur, the marches and demonstrations were drawing attention to animal cruelty on many levels, including the clubbing of seals, the mistreatment of animals in captivity, and the horrors conducted in the name of medical research. The antifur movement is dear to my heart, but our protests had a ripple effect across all animal rights issues.

As the movement grew and I participated in the marches, I received stacks of mail. We were making a difference. Fur sales dropped. People stopped buying them. We wanted to make people feel embarrassed and humiliated to be seen wearing fur, and we succeeded.

My association with the beauty pageants was a positive one. Though it came to an end because of my concern for animals, that does not mean I did not love the experience with the pageants. I traveled all over the world. I worked with wonderfully dedicated professionals, and beautiful young ladies from many countries of the world. It was a pleasure and an honor to be involved with Miss USA and Miss Universe for so many years.

12

Touching Bases
from *Happy Gilmore*
to the Rose Parade

I spent more than fifty years on television, but I appeared in only one film and that was *Happy Gilmore*. It was released in 1996, and I appear in the movie for only a few minutes, but that brief appearance proved to be hugely popular, especially with young men. I did *The Price Is Right* for more than ten years after that movie, and to the last day, I never taped a show that someone in the audience did not bring up *Happy Gilmore* and my role in the picture. I had no idea how popular that film—and that fight—would become.

Happy Gilmore was a comedy starring Adam Sandler. He was not only the star of the picture, he was also a writer and one of the producers. He wrote that bit in the movie for me, without ever telling me or talking with me about it. He just wrote it. In the scene, Adam Sandler's character, Happy Gilmore, gets into a fight with me on a golf course. It is all played for laughs as he wrote it. When Adam had a finished script, he sent it to my public relations representative, Henri Bollinger, and asked if I would do it.

I read the script, and when I discovered that I won the fight, I knew I wanted to do it. I had studied karate for eight years with Chuck Norris before he became a movie star. For eight years, Chuck had beaten me up twice a week, and at long last I had an opportunity to win a fight. I didn't wait for opportunity to knock twice. I said, "Yes!"

We went up to Canada to shoot the movie on a golf course outside of Vancouver. It rained at least part of every day, and there I was, out there in the wet grass, wrestling with Adam. The weather was so wet that we had to shoot whenever we could. I remember thinking: "Here I am, seventy-three years old, rolling around in the wet grass with this young man, and I am bound to catch pneumonia." But I didn't even catch a cold. We shot the scene in about three days. I thought it was fun, a thoroughly enjoyable experience, but I had no idea it would gain cult status with a huge number of moviegoers.

Dennis Dugan, the director, said they had a stuntman who would do as much of the fighting as I thought necessary. I didn't say so to Dennis, but I thought: "Oh, no. I've come all the way up here to Canada to win a fight. Not to watch a stuntman win it." To Dennis, I said, "I know how to fight. I'll do it myself." Dennis said OK, but he looked genuinely surprised—after all, I was seventy-three years old.

Adam did all his fighting, too. When I knocked him into that pond, it was Adam himself who went in. The only time we used stuntmen was for the long roll down the hill, and one of the stuntmen hurt his back doing it. Frequently people, particularly young men, ask me if I could beat up Adam Sandler in real life. I say, "Are you kidding? Adam Sandler couldn't whip Regis Philbin." Interestingly, I've tried Pat Sajak and Alex Trebek in that line, but Regis always gets the biggest laugh. Why?

I also went to the premiere with Adam Sandler. We pulled up to the theater at Universal Studios in a golf cart, which was appropriate because our brawl occurred on a golf course. It was at the premiere that I got the first inkling of what the public's reaction to our fight would be. After the screening, there was a big party at Universal, and people were pounding me on the back, congratulating me, and telling me how much they enjoyed seeing me punch out Adam.

If you saw *Happy Gilmore,* you will recall that at one stage in the fight, Adam clobbers me and then says, "The price is wrong, bitch." At the end of the fight, I finish off Adam and walk away saying, "Now you've had enough." Then I pause and turn to say: "Bitch." That line became *the* line so far as our *The Price Is Right* audiences were concerned.

After the movie was released, I never taped a show that someone in the audience didn't bring up *Happy Gilmore.* And, within minutes, members of the audience were asking me to do *the* line. Of course, I refused. I told them that line was acting of the highest order. I don't talk that way in real life—which made the audience only more demanding. "Do the line! Do the line!" they shouted from every corner of the studio. Sometimes the entire audience would begin chanting: "Do the line."

I would finally say, "Well, I am going to ask our associate producer Kathy Greco." Kathy would always be sitting at a desk near the set, and I would tell them: "If she says I can say the line, then I will say it. But if she says no, then I can't say it."

And so they would start yelling at her, "Come on, Kathy. Come on, Kathy!"

"Now leave her alone," I would say, but they would yell and scream and plead with her.

Finally, I would say, "Kathy, these people want me to say, 'Now you've had enough. . . . Bitch,' but I don't think I should."

And the audience would explode in laughter and screaming.

Or I would get a signal from the stage manager, who would tell me we had thirty seconds before we went on the air, and the audience would be begging me to say the phrase. I would say, "No, I am sorry, we do not have enough time. I do not have the time to say it."

Then I would get another signal from the stage manager, ten seconds, nine seconds, and at the last moment right before we went on, I would say, "I don't have enough time to say, 'Now you've had enough. . . . Bitch.'"

And the audience would roar with laughter as we went on air.

Adam Sandler is a talented man, and he was a pleasure to work with on the film. Later on, in 2007 when CBS did a prime-time special for my fiftieth anniversary on television, he came on the show and we had a lot of fun together. We showed a clip from *Happy Gilmore,* and he wrote a poem about me that was hilarious. He read the poem on the show, and it got great laughs.

Shortly after my retirement, I was inducted into the National Association of Broadcasters Hall of Fame. The Hall of Fame committee requested that we provide a tape, a sort of *This Is Your Life, Bob Barker* for the occasion, and Adam Sandler took time from what I know to be a very busy schedule to narrate the tape.

Adam's career has been a thing to behold since *Happy Gilmore*. But if his kindnesses to me are any indication, he remains the same sincere, thoughtful young man I had the pleasure of working with in Canada more than ten years ago.

. . .

Over the years, I made other television appearances besides *Truth* and *Price*. Nothing dramatic, usually as myself, but I did log quite a few appearances on a variety of talk shows, game shows, and a few sitcoms. I did an episode of *Bonanza* in 1960. I remember I stole a girl from Little Joe. Not many men can make that claim!

Dorothy Jo and I appeared together on a few game shows that had married couples on them. We did *Tattletales* several times. That was a show where wives and husbands would predict their spouses' reactions to various questions. They kept inviting us back because they thought Dorothy Jo was hilarious. I resented it. *Tattletales* was hosted by Bert Convy, a nice man who died too young.

I was also on *Match Game* quite a bit—there were tons of laughs on that show. Richard Dawson was a panelist with whom I was so impressed that later on I hired him as the host of a local television show I produced called *Lucky Pair*. I tried to sell it in syndication, but I was never able to cut it. It was a good show, too, based on an idea of my mother's.

Lucky Pair was a board game played by two contestants.

The contestant who completed the most pairs won the game. To complete a pair you had to match two squares on the board. A contestant chose a number on the board, the square turned around, and perhaps it might reveal "1492." The contestant would say, "Columbus discovered America," and complete a pair. But suppose a square revealed "Civil War general" and the contestant said, "Robert E. Lee," and the square turned back into place. That was not the answer we were looking for—the pair was not completed.

Now, the contestant should try to remember the number of the "Civil War general" square in case he discovers the square that reads "General James Longstreet." Think about it for a moment. *Lucky Pair* offered endless possibilities that were a lot of fun.

Geoff Edwards was the first host of *Lucky Pair*. We auditioned a dozen hosts for the job, and I told the folks at CBS that Geoff was the man. But there were several doubters. I talked them into giving Geoff a chance, and in a couple of weeks, everyone wanted to take credit for hiring him. He was that good.

He left *Lucky Pair* when he got an opportunity to do a network show with his wife. That's when we hired Richard Dawson. I've hired two hosts, Geoff and Richard. I'd say I'm batting a thousand.

• • •

In the 1970s, I was a frequent guest on *The Dinah Shore Show*. Dinah taped right down the hall from *Price* for years. When a guest dropped out, they called me. As a result, I was on her show more than any other guest. They even talked with me about cohosting with Dinah, but Sol, my agent, nixed that. He thought I'd be spreading myself too thin.

Craig Ferguson, the late-night talk show host at CBS, has had me on his show a couple of times. He keeps telling his audience that I am a vampire. I don't know how he found out.

I've been on *The Late Show* with David Letterman. I've done Conan O'Brien's show. I did Rosie O'Donnell's show. Every time I went to New York, I was on her show. We had a lot of fun. She always said when I retired, she wanted to replace me, and when I retired, she did talk to the producers. But I think she wanted to move the show to New York. That was not going to happen.

I did the *Ellen DeGeneres Show*. She is a charming host. I received the Emmy for Best Host the year that I retired, and Ellen followed me to the podium. She said she intended to add more controversy to her own show, and she was going to start that very night by saying, "I think Bob Barker is a quitter."

• • •

In 1996, I did a couple of episodes of a sitcom called *Something So Right,* which starred Mel Harris. I played her father, and Shirley Jones played her mother. Shirley and I were separated but still involved. It was a funny show.

Not only had I never been in a sitcom, but in all honesty, I had not watched sitcoms enough to really get the feel of them. So here I was, cast in *Something So Right,* and worried that I was about to do something so wrong. We started rehearsals, and it did not take Shirley Jones long to realize that I did not know what I was doing. But she helped me tremendously. Between takes and segment rehearsals, she and I would sit down and she would go over my lines with me. She taught me that in sitcoms, everything moves fast. The speech is fast. You say a line. I say a line. He says a line, and *boom, boom, boom.* I just tried to keep up to speed with the rest of the cast.

But it went well, and they had me back. I did two of those shows with Shirley, and she was such a gracious lady. I will always be very grateful to her. She was my dialogue coach, and to have an Academy Award winner as your dialogue coach is the way to go. The very talented producers, Judd Pillot and John Peaslee, were a joy to work with, too.

. . .

Having Shirley Jones as my dialogue coach was like having Chuck Norris as my karate instructor, which incidentally, is what I had also. Chuck was a guest on *Truth or Consequences.* He was a karate champion, and he came on and did a demonstration on the show. Not only had I never done karate, I had never seen it. But I was so impressed by Chuck that I started taking lessons. Chuck and I became friends, and I introduced him to a fellow I knew at Metromedia television, hoping to get him started with a television show. It did not work out, but we continued to be friends, and of course he went on to huge success.

After Chuck's first appearance on the show, he came back and did another demonstration. This time I chose three contestants, three women out of the audience, and told them they were going to learn some karate from Chuck Norris. It was a joke on the whole audience. I chose young women who looked fit. We had a mat, and Chuck said, "OK, lady number one, come over here and I'll show you how to throw a punch." He did that and then maybe a kick or two, and then he showed her how to throw him down. Then lady number two went through these basic things, and he showed her how to defend herself. Now when he starts with lady number three—she kicks him, hits him, and throws him up over her shoulder. He's flopping all over the place, and she's really in command. The audience was screaming. Lady number three was actually Chuck's wife. We had planted her in the audience, and she knew some karate. It was a hilarious spot to see this woman pummeling the karate champion.

It was the beginning of a lifetime friendship with Chuck Norris. He became my first karate teacher. He used to come over to my house and give me lessons. We worked out on the lawn at first, but later on I stopped putting my car in the garage, and I had the garage floor all padded and made it a karate studio. I had a big mirror put in so I could see my chops and kicks, and he and I worked together for eight years.

Chuck taught what might be described as the Chuck Norris version of the Tang Soo Do karate style. Tang Soo Do is basically foot fighting, but Chuck taught hand techniques aplenty. I became a red belt, which is just below black belt. Chuck always wanted to test me for black belt, but I declined. I have so much respect for the black belt rank that I would rather be a pretty good red belt than a marginal black belt.

When Chuck's movie career took off, I started studying with Pat Johnson, who was a fighter on one of Chuck's karate teams and a stuntman. He and I worked together for several years. I started late in life, but I thoroughly enjoyed karate. You have to be stretched out, really loose. Chuck got me into a regular exercise schedule, and that was so important. I was in karate for twenty-one years, and I still exercise regularly, thanks to my friends Chuck and Pat.

That reminds me of a story regarding Chuck Norris and his brother, Aaron. It involved my mother, too. Chuck was over at my house, and we were sparring. He kicked me in the side. It hurt, and it continued to hurt. A few days later his brother, Aaron, came over. We were sparring, and he punched me in the other side with his fist. That hurt, too, and continued to hurt. Finally, I went to the doctor. I told him I was struck here and here and I was still hurting. After he looked at some X-rays the doctor said, "I'm not surprised you are still hurting. You have two cracked ribs here, and another two cracked ribs here, and I would expect both places to hurt."

I came home, and I told my mother, who was living with us then, that Chuck had cracked two of my ribs and that his brother Aaron had cracked two ribs on the other side.

My mom said, "I think you're going to have to stop playing with those Norris boys."

• • •

Beginning in the early 1980s, I began to go on the road regularly with an audience participation show playing in large-scale venues around the country. While the format was everything I was accustomed to doing—that is, games, prizes, audience participation, and plenty of ad-libbing and improvisation—the sheer size of the audiences made these shows a completely different entertainment challenge. Much to my delight, it was a hugely successful format, and I went on to do these traveling shows for eight years. We broke records for attendance, and within a short time, we would only book arenas that could seat at least ten thousand people. We often played to audiences of twenty thousand. We smashed records all over the country. It was great fun playing to such enthusiastic large crowds everywhere.

These live stage shows started innocently enough with a phone call to my agent, Sol Leon. There were a couple of men—a dentist named Dr. Robert Rowe and his friend, Sheldon Ferguson, an attorney—who were associated with a charity and wanted me to do a fund-raiser. They contacted Sol Leon, who represented me at the William Morris Agency.

Sol told me, "I got a phone call and this fellow is talking about some pretty good money. He wants you to come down to Johnson City, Tennessee, and do a show."

I asked Sol what sort of show the caller was talking about.

"I don't know," he said. "Why don't you talk to him and see if you are interested."

So I called Dr. Rowe and asked him, "What do you want me to do?"

He said, "Just do what you always do."

I said, "I talk with people, play games, and give away prizes."

Dr. Rowe said, "That's what I want you to do."

And that is how it all started. I asked Dr. Rowe if he could get some people to help me, and he said that he could get all the members of the Johnson City Kiwanis Club. I suggested that a show like that might benefit from a couple of pretty girls on the stage, and he said he would not only get a few pretty girls, he would get some beauty queens. Then I asked if he could get some prizes, and he said, "Oh, yes, the merchants are eager to cooperate, and there will be plenty of prizes." He was very optimistic and had answers for everything.

So I told him that I would write a script in great detail, describing every movement that had to be made, and I would send a copy to him. "Then," I said, "I am going to get on the phone and go over that script with you. If you can get this all together, I will come down and do your show." So that is what we did. I described every game, every prize, every prop. The responsibilities of stagehands and models were all laid out. I asked him to tell his workers to do exactly what we had discussed, everything I had written down, and to have everything set to do the show. I told him I would come in the day before the show, and we would rehearse everything very carefully that night.

He said, "That is fine. We will be ready." He was completely confident.

Up to this point the show seemed to be all set, but when I got on the airplane to go to Tennessee, the weather in that part of the country was terrible. We could not get near Johnson City, Tennessee. It was a fierce winter storm. I ended up in Kansas City, Missouri, that Friday night. The show was scheduled for Saturday night. So I called Dr. Rowe, and he said, "Hello, Bob, where are you?"

I said, "I don't want you to worry because everything is going to be fine, but I am in Kansas City."

There was a long pause.

"Dr. Rowe?" I said.

In a dazed voice, Dr. Rowe asked, "What are you doing in Kansas City?"

I explained the weather problem and assured him that they had told me I would be able to get in tomorrow. "If you can meet me at the airport, we will go directly to the venue," I said. "We'll put this show together and it will work."

The next day, the weather was again horrendous, but I did manage to arrive in Tennessee. By the time we left the airport, it was close to showtime. I was happy to discover that Dr. Rowe and his crew of fifteen men and two young ladies were all prepared. I had told them every move to make, right down to the last detail, in the script, and they were on top of it. They were like a veteran Hollywood crew, sharp and dedicated, and they wanted to work.

We did the show, despite a veritable blizzard in the area, and we filled Jefferson Hall. We had an audience of eight thousand people and turned away a couple of thousand more. The show was a smash hit. They laughed, screamed, and applauded, and they gave me a standing ovation at the end. After the show, Dr. Rowe came up to me and said in his rich southern accent, "I think you ought to be doing more of these shows."

And I said, "I think you are right."

That was how the live road show began, and it became wildly popular. We broke the record at the Omni in Atlanta. We filled the Summit in Cincinnati. Everywhere we went, we sold out and broke attendance records. I was still hosting *The Price Is Right* in Hollywood, but I would fly out on Thursday or Friday, do a show Friday night and then do another one in a nearby city on Saturday night. I would jump on a plane and fly back on Sunday and go to work on *Price* on Monday.

Dr. Rowe and Sheldon Ferguson had a company called the Tennessee Partners that promoted country-and-western acts—and as of that night, Bob Barker. We started barnstorming all over the map. We went on a tear that lasted eight years. You name it, we played it: Omaha, Oklahoma City, Seattle, Cleveland, Detroit, Tampa, Miami, and Atlanta. We went all over. They wanted us to play Madison Square Garden in New York, but the advertising costs were outrageous, and I did not want to do a show that would just pay for advertising. They wanted us to play at the old Los Angeles Forum, but I didn't want to appear at the Forum because we taped *The Price Is Right* in Los Angeles. I thought if people wanted to come see me in Los Angeles, they could come see me for free doing *The Price Is Right*.

Dr. Rowe was the one who suggested that we call the show *The Bob Barker Fun and Games Show*.

I said, "You got it."

When I first started doing *The Bob Barker Fun and Games Show* live in front of such large audiences, I thought we might have to have big acts with lots of things happening on the stage. Not so. I learned that folks loved to have me roam through the audience, even up into the balcony.

The lighting man would follow me with a spot as I had fun with people of all ages and colors, even with kids as young as four or five. I'd pick them up, stand them on their chairs and stay with a youngster as long as we were getting laughs. I remember talking with a six-year-old boy in San Antonio for about five minutes. The audience loved him.

If I was in the balcony, I sometimes chose a contestant seated on the floor below, in which case the lighting man threw a second spot on the contestant. With me in the balcony and the contestant seated on the floor below, we would play a game mounted on a board on the stage.

The two-hour show had a *Hellzapoppin'* atmosphere. The audience didn't know where I would be next or who I might be talking with, but, of course, they hoped it would be with them. And the best part was, it just might have been!

Sounds like fun, doesn't it? Believe me, it was. I think I enjoyed the show as much as anyone in the audience, even the contestant who won the car at the end of the show.

Sol Leon came out two or three times to see *The Bob Barker Fun and Games Show*. Once he said, "Bob, this is the nearest thing to the Beatles I ever saw." I know, I know: Sol was my agent, but it still sounded good to me.

When we were going into a city to do a show, the Tennessee Partners would lay out a complete advertising plan—newspapers, radio, and television. Then they would send it to Sol. Sol would look the plan over very carefully, and he always made suggestions, made changes, and added valuable insights.

At this time, Sol was having breakfast once a week with the legendary Colonel Tom Parker, who promoted all of Elvis Presley's personal appearances. Sol said the Colonel became interested in *The Bob Barker Fun and Games Show* and gave him tips from time to time on promoting the show. I think you'll agree that Sol was getting tips from an excellent source.

People often told me that my relationship with Sol Leon was something to behold, and it was. He was my agent, but he was far more than that. He was an advertising consultant, an advisor, and a dear friend.

. . .

The Bob Barker Fun and Games Show was not the only traveling show I was doing during those days, nor was it the only other job I had outside of *The Price Is Right.* I was hosting the annual beauty pageants. I was also anchoring the Rose Parade broadcasts every year for CBS. In fact, I was involved with a number of parades around the country. I did the Macy's Thanksgiving Day Parade in New York and the Mummers Parade in Philadelphia. For years, I worked the Indianapolis 500 Festival Parade. But the granddaddy of them all, as they say, is the Tournament of Roses Parade in Pasadena. That was a privilege and a pleasure for me to do for over twenty years.

I worked with some wonderful people when I narrated the Rose Parade. I cohosted shows with June Lockhart. She was one bright lady, and she was funny. I worked with Joan Van Ark, who was bright and funny, too. As I wrote earlier, I interviewed the grand marshals every year. One time it was Charles Schulz, the creator of *Peanuts,* and I am a big fan. I knew he did not like to give autographs, but once when he and I were alone, I apologetically requested one. He quickly sketched Snoopy on my script, wrote, "To Bob with friendship and affection," and signed it "Sparky," a nickname his friends called him. It is one of my treasures.

Because of the Rose Parade, for twenty-one years I was unable to go to a New Year's Eve party. I had to be out there in Pasadena at 4:00 a.m. They really took it seriously. Our team would go to Pasadena for two days or so before the parade. We taped the places where they built the floats and interviewed the float builders. We did a lot of research about the parade, and we studied up on the background of the groups marching in the parade.

I have anchored parades all over the country, but the Rose Parade is the best-organized parade of them all. If they say they are going to step off at 8:00 a.m., you can set your watch by it. And if they say a band will pass the reviewing stand at 9:15, you can bet that band will be there, playing its best music, at 9:15. Many parades do not operate that way.

The Rose Parade in Pasadena definitely has better weather for a parade than any other place in the country. So many of these big parades are around the holidays, and if you are in the East, say New York or Cleveland or Detroit, the weather can be atrocious. I know. I have been there.

I did the Indianapolis 500 Festival Parade for twenty-one years. (Have you noticed that twenty-one seems to be my favorite number? As Dorothy Jo noted, I am nothing if not tenacious!) I made many friends in Indianapolis, and I enjoyed the annual visit. The race-car drivers were always a fun bunch, and after the parade we would go to the race, which was even more exciting.

* * *

It was John Christ who steered me to the Rose Parade job that I thoroughly enjoyed for twenty-one years, who hired me to do the Miss USA and the Miss Universe beauty pageants, which I did for twenty-one years, and finally, who hired me to host the Pillsbury Bake-Off every year. He was the agency representative for Pillsbury at the Leo Burnett Agency. He called me one day and said, "We need a producer and a host." He asked if I would be willing to both produce and host the bake-off.

Without hesitation, I said, "Sure. Why not?" I knew nothing about the bake-off, but I learned, and I hosted that contest for twenty years. (Somehow I missed my usual twenty-one!)

The only thing I didn't like about the bake-off was taking off the weight I always gained. You see, I got to taste the entries!

John Christ had a wonderful sense of humor, and we could talk for hours together. I remember we were sitting on a plane in the mid-1960s, and we were trying to decide what to drink. I knew he liked screwdrivers, and about this time there was a popular new drink called a Harvey Wallbanger. It was vodka, orange juice, and Galliano. I said, "John, I have never had a Harvey Wallbanger, but I think it has some of the ingredients of a screwdriver."

He said, "Let's try some Harvey Wallbangers."

So we started drinking them. We talked and laughed as always, and we were solving all the problems of television and advertising. Eventually, I looked up and everybody on the airplane was standing up in the aisle.

I said to John, "What's going on here? Look at these people."

"I don't know what is going on," he replied.

I asked a gentleman in the aisle what was happening.

The gentleman gave me a look of amazement and said, "This airplane has been struck by lightning."

Everybody was frightened and they were all on their feet, but John and I had not even noticed.

John, however, handled the situation perfectly. He turned to a flight attendant and said, "Miss, could we have two more Harvey Wallbangers, please?"

13

DJ&T Foundation

I have had animals around me since I was a small child. I have always felt deeply for animals. While I was growing up on the Rosebud Indian Reservation in Mission, South Dakota, as I have mentioned, my mother could look out from the rooftop of the two-story hotel where we lived and was able to find me by looking for the pack of dogs that would always be following me.

. . .

One aspect of my animal activism has been my constant reminders for people to have their pets spayed or neutered. For years and years, I ended every *The Price Is Right* show with the words "Help control the pet population. Have your pets spayed or neutered." Pet overpopulation is a huge problem, and we have much further to go, but I am proud to have played a part in raising awareness. Every little bit helps. Despite growing awareness, people still have no conception of the magnitude of the pet overpopulation problem.

There are almost a million animals taken in by shelters each year in California alone, cats and dogs, and of that million, half of them are euthanized every year. In addition to the cruelty factor, it is also costing taxpayers $250 million a year to capture the animals, house them, kill them, and then dispose of them. It is nothing less than a travesty. And with education, it can be stopped. That is why I have worked so hard for so many years. These things can be improved. Changes can happen. I have seen progress on many fronts, and it is part of what keeps me working to help educate others and campaign for new laws, education, and overall awareness.

Along with many others, I have worked to encourage cities, states, and various local governments to institute mandatory spay/neuter laws and ordinances. This would do a great deal to cut down on the tragic stray dog and feral cat problem. Many of these strays and ferals suffer unbearably during their lifetimes. They contract diseases. They are injured, attacked, hit by cars, sold into research, and worse. Most people are not aware of the extent of animal suffering. Americans do, by and large, love animals. According to the U.S. Census Bureau statistics, 63 percent of all homes in the United States include at least one animal.

People love their own cats and dogs, but when it comes to awareness, most people just have no conception of the animal cruelty problems that exist in this country. That is what I and many other passionately committed people in various organizations are working toward: increasing awareness. Increased awareness leads to increased activism, and increased activism leads to discussion and behavior changes and ultimately to new laws and more stringent enforcement of the laws already on the books.

While I have become involved in all kinds of animal rights causes, the spay/neuter issue is my main advocacy project. In memory of my wife Dorothy Jo and my mother Matilda (Tilly), who were both devoted animal lovers, I established the DJ&T Foundation, which is a nonprofit organization that subsidizes low-cost spay/neuter clinics and voucher programs throughout the country. It was established in 1994, and since then, the DJ&T Foundation has contributed millions of dollars to fund clinics and programs which provide spay/neuter services. The DJ&T Foundation offers grants to organizations across the country that meet the foundation's criteria.

If being on television all these years has helped to make it possible for me to reach people with an important message about animals, then by all means I am going to use that visibility and opportunity. When I received the Lifetime Achievement Award for Daytime Television, I closed my remarks by saying, "Have your pets spayed or neutered." When I was inducted into the Television Hall of Fame, I said I supposed that I was expected to say something profound and I would. I said, "Help control the pet population. Have your pets spayed or neutered." At Drury University, I received an honorary doctorate, and I was privileged to give the commencement address. I closed that speech by advising the graduates to "help control the pet population. Have your pets spayed or neutered." Of course, I got a laugh. But better still, I made a point.

Activists across the country are working on new legislation

in support of mandatory spay/neuter programs. Some states have already passed such laws, and others provide funding for people to get their pets spayed or neutered when they don't have money for the surgery. Mandatory spaying or neutering is gaining more and more momentum, and where laws have been implemented, the results are very encouraging. In Santa Cruz County, here in California, for instance, a mandatory spay/neuter program was implemented. In ten years, while the human population in Santa Cruz County increased by 15 percent, the number of animals—cats and dogs—turned in at shelters decreased 60 percent. That is very impressive.

Spaying and neutering is so obviously the solution to the tragic overpopulation problem that one would just instinctively believe that we would not run into opposition. Everyone loves animals, right? But believe me, there are powerful lobbies, groups, and industries that have launched serious opposition to the animal rights causes in which I have become involved. If you trace the opposition through all the little channels, eventually you find it is always based on greed.

One group opposing the mandatory spay/neuter program is the breeders. There are legitimate breeders, and their business will not be impeded, but there are also all the backyard breeders and puppy mill operators, many of whom are not licensed and pay no taxes, and they are contributing to the tragic overpopulation problem. Some veterinarians oppose anything that will reduce the size of the animal population. It comes down to business, and it comes down to greed. The fewer the animals, the fewer the patients. It is disgusting.

Again, in most cases, whether it is the fur industry, vivisection, or even the entertainment industry, animal abuse is the result of greed. And when you care about the animals as much as I do and as much as so many others do, it is totally unacceptable to see the poor animals paying the price for unsavory human avarice. Invariably, the people who vigorously oppose suggestions that would improve life for animals are people who in some way profit from the exploitation of animals. Breeders, research scientists, animal trainers, farmers, and the movie industry are just some of the groups from which offenders come. And let's add circuses, rodeos, roadside shows, and zoos to the list.

. . .

Some of the most egregious animal abuse has always resided in the field of animal experimentation, often conducted at top universities around the country. In many cases, these experiments are essentially animal torture and senseless mutilation. I am vehemently opposed to vivisection, and I have spoken out against it for years. I have participated in protests and marches. I have written letters, given speeches, and tried whenever I could to shine a light on the barbaric experiments done on animals of various kinds.

For years, animals were used in tests for cosmetics and household products. These animals were subjected to blinding, poisoning, and skin infections of all kinds. The test results were useless. They resulted in inaccuracies and were dangerous to human health. Animals and humans are different. The test results are inconclusive. I am delighted to see more and more companies turning their backs on animal testing and pointing it out to consumers on labels and in advertising.

Animal researchers have historically done some horrendous

experiments. I do not want to go into all the gory details, but it is animal torture. There is no other word for it. These researchers know what they are doing to the animals. They know it is barbaric. And they do it anyway. It all comes down to money. They get millions of dollars in federal grants to do animal experiments. One of the easiest ways to get a federal grant is to perform animal experiments. We have been pleading for years with the NIH (National Institutes of Health) to back off, but they continue to sanction—and in some cases demand—animal experiments.

One of the great tragedies is that many of these tests are redundant—the identical tests are done over and over at several different universities. It is sickening to think of the senseless, repetitive, and useless torture being conducted. It is also a complete waste of taxpayer money. The same researchers repeatedly receive these federal grants; "research welfare," it is often called. It is a difficult problem to attack, but we are attacking it. And I think we have made progress. There have been signs that we are having an impact. For example, primate experiments have been considerably reduced. I think that by highlighting these atrocities, the animal rights movement has reduced the level of cruelty to animals in the laboratory, but it is an ongoing battle.

• • •

I have mentioned Nancy Burnet several times in this book, and well I should. But before I continue further, I'd like to explain how she came into my life. In 1983, I was at an animal shelter in Orange County for an event, the purpose of which was to attract a crowd, and hopefully, find homes for some of the shelter's dogs. The day was drawing to a close, and I was trying to find a quality home for a dog I had on a leash.

I looked across the shelter yard and saw Nancy as she arrived. I thought: "There is one great-looking lady." As I said, the day was drawing to a close, so I didn't have time to waste. I went over to her, introduced myself, and explained that I was trying to find a good home for the dog I had on the leash. Then I asked her if she was married or single.

Looking a bit startled, Nancy replied, "I am just winding up a divorce."

I said, "Good! Then this dog is definitely for you, and I will have to come over to your home on weekends and occasionally during the week to check on him." Nancy adopted the dog, and in the years to come, there were times when she got along with the dog much better than she got along with me. Actually, Nancy and I have a long list of things in common, not the least of which is that she doesn't intend to marry again. Nor do I. Our relationship has gone on for twenty-five years, off and on. Mostly on.

Nancy is a very brave and knowledgeable woman who has played an important role in the animal rights movement. She is the founder and director of United Activists for Animal Rights, which is headquartered in Riverside, California, but she works on animal projects from coast to coast. In addition to all Nancy accomplishes with UAAR, she is a valuable and respected part of the DJ&T Foundation's success. As executive director, she interviews the applicants for grants, and I know of no one else so well qualified to handle that assignment. Using Nancy's notes, the board of directors makes its decisions on the grant requests. But she also has the knowledge and background to advise the grantees in the operation of their organizations. We have a file full of letters from executives of organizations expressing their gratitude for Nancy's assistance in solving problems of every description.

Nancy Burnet, who has not always received the credit that she so richly deserves for her stellar work on behalf of animals, has worked tirelessly to protect animals in entertainment, where they are frequently beaten, starved, and mistreated miserably in order to make them perform. One of the more publicized incidents in which we became involved was the exposé of animal cruelty in the production of a movie called *Project X*, which used chimpanzees. The moviemakers had gone to one of the world's foremost primatologists, Dr. Roger Fouts, dean of graduate studies and research at Central Washington University and codirector of the Chimpanzee and Human Communication Institute. They wanted to get Roger involved with the film. They showed the script to him. He looked over what they wanted the chimps to do and told the moviemakers: "You cannot do this. You cannot possibly do this without beating the chimps. You should use actors in chimp outfits, or you should work in a different direction, but do not use live chimps."

They insisted on using live chimps, and he said he would not have anything to do with the picture. Roger walked out, but they went ahead with their plan.

Nancy and I were informed that there was a great deal of animal cruelty on the set of the film. We were told in graphic detail that the trainers were beating the chimps with clubs, fists, and blackjacks. We heard all kinds of horror stories about what was happening on the set, so we got on the phone and started making some calls to responsible people.

Eventually, we got the city of Los Angeles involved, and by the time the city finished its investigation, the city wanted to file animal cruelty charges against the animal trainers who worked on the picture. The trainers avoided actual prosecution because the statute of limitations had run out, but the investigation and accusations made against the animal trainers and producers received vast media attention nationwide.

I have been told that the *Project X* exposé probably did more to make the public aware of the cruelty to animals in the production of movies than anything else has ever done. To this day, whenever someone hears *Project X*, they think of the chimps and the cruelty involved with the filming of that movie. Score one for the Burnet/Barker duo!

After the *Project X* exposé, Nancy placed ads in the trade papers urging people on sets who observed animal mistreatment to contact UAAR. Of course, people who reported cruelty to animals on sets were promised anonymity. Otherwise, they risked losing their jobs or even being blackballed in the industry. It was as a result of these ads that Nancy received a telephone call regarding the television show *Dr. Quinn, Medicine Woman*. The caller reported that horses used on *Dr. Quinn, Medicine Woman* were not receiving proper care. Eventually, Nancy found a second eyewitness who confirmed the first report.

Nancy and I discussed how we should proceed. As a result of our experience with the American Humane Association during the *Project X* exposé, we had lost all confidence in AHA. We decided to seek the assistance of Madeline Bernstein of SPCALA, who has a rock-solid reputation for having no sympathy for animal abusers. We called Madeline, told her what the two eyewitnesses had reported, and asked her if she would meet with us and discuss the matter. Typical of Madeline, she said, "There's no need for further discussion. I'll have two humane officers out there tomorrow in plainclothes to check it out." The two humane officers checked out everything having to do with the horses and reported that conditions were as bad as—if not worse than—the eyewitnesses had described them to be.

Beth Sullivan, executive producer of *Dr. Quinn, Medicine Woman,* emerged as a heroine. She told the humane officers that she had been concerned about the horses and had told the head wrangler to take better care of them. In spite of the fact that Beth Sullivan agreed with SPCALA humane officers that a problem existed with the manner in which the horses had been cared for and that the problem had to be corrected, the woman who at that time was the director of the American Humane Association Hollywood office went on television and said that AHA had two officers on duty at all times, and they had observed no problems with the horses. Can you understand why Nancy and I don't go to the American Humane Association with animal abuse problems in movies and on television?

• • •

In regards to legislation, it was in the late 1980s that I had a telephone call from Marion La Folette, who was a California assemblywoman at that time. Marion said that she wanted to amend the California penal code to include felony penalties for animal abusers who commit crimes against animals. As the penal code was written at that time, such crimes were only a misdemeanor. Marion asked me if I would be willing to come to Sacramento to lobby in favor of such an amendment. I said, "Gladly. Crimes against animals should be a felony."

Marion said, "Thank you, Bob, and you can write the language for the amendment."

I told Marion that writing the language for the amendment was not my bag, but that I had a friend who could do it beautifully. Of course, I was referring to Nancy Burnet, who has extensive experience in such writing. As it turned out, Nancy not only wrote the language for the amendment to the penal code but also managed to close some loopholes in the code along the way. Nancy wrote the amendment and lobbied. I lobbied, too. Marion got the amendment passed and, as a result, an animal abuser who commits a crime against an animal in the state of California has committed a felony.

For a quarter of a century, I have had the good fortune and the pleasure of working with Nancy Burnet and her organization, United Activists for Animal Rights, in an effort to make ours a better world for animals. Animal rights activists across the country—around the world, as a matter of fact—have accomplished a great deal and the momentum increases almost daily. As Al Jolson used to say: "You ain't seen nothing yet!"

14

Retirement Can Keep You Busy

I am a complete success at retirement.

I think I stopped doing *The Price Is Right* at just the right time. I enjoyed hosting right up to the last minute of the last show. But I had been concerned that the first morning that I awakened and realized that I didn't have a show to do that day—or ever—I might go into a deep depression or at least a funk.

However, quite the contrary, I awakened with a wonderful feeling of relaxation. I had enjoyed doing my shows so very much for half a century that it had never occurred to me that my demanding schedule for so many years might have had any adverse affect on me whatsoever. But since my retirement, I am so much more relaxed, both physically and mentally, that there is no doubt that I chose to retire at just the right time—not too late, not too soon.

Please don't picture me sitting around staring off into space, doing nothing. I do plan to do some of that, if I ever get time. Actually, I feel as if I am starting a new, completely different, and very exciting phase of my life, one that I hope will be productive and pleasing to others, as well as to me.

* * *

As I write, I have been retired from *Price* for more than a year. One of the things that has kept me busy is writing this book. I had been approached several times over the years by agents who wanted me to write a book, but when I announced my retirement, I received an attractive offer from one of the top publishers. I accepted, but before we could sign the papers, the deal collapsed, through no fault of mine or the publisher.

Norman Brokaw, chairman of the board of the famous William Morris Agency, and I have known each other since Sol Leon was solving all my problems. When I told Norman that my book deal was no more, Norman promptly said, "Bob, I'll get you a publisher if you want to write a book."

I said, "I'm not sure I want to. Let me think about it."

About a week later, while I was thinking about it, Norman called and said, "Bob, I have an excellent offer for you from an excellent publisher."

"I guess I am going to write a book," I said. And, you know, I have thoroughly enjoyed writing this book. To me, it's a lot like talking to an audience. Of course, I'm writing about me, and I've always liked talking about myself.

Dorothy Jo and I used to have what we called chat time. At the end of the day, before dinner, we'd sit down, I'd pour a couple of glasses of wine, and we would chat. One evening we sat down, I poured our wine, and Dorothy Jo said, "Barker, tonight let's talk about anything but you."

I couldn't think of a thing to say.

Dorothy Jo was a very funny lady, often at my expense. One time she was being interviewed by a newspaper reporter who asked, "How have you and Bob remained happily married for so long—particularly here in Hollywood, where so many people go through one divorce after another?"

Dorothy Jo thought for a moment and answered: "Our marriage is based on love. I love Barker, and Barker loves Barker." Dorothy Jo had to pour her own wine that evening, and I talked about myself during our chat time.

As I recall these remarks of Dorothy Jo's, I am reminded that I haven't written anything as yet about the grand old house that we bought in 1969 when we moved back to Hollywood from the San Fernando Valley and in which I sit as I write.

The first home built in Hollywood, an adobe, was located on the lot on which our house now stands. Eventually, Harrison Gray Otis, founder of the *Los Angeles Times,* bought the adobe. He named it the Outpost and lived in it until he died.

Our house was built in 1929. It's a Spanish Colonial Revival style with the original tile in all the bathrooms, leaded windows, stained-glass windows, a hand-carved padre's walk (balcony) the length of the house, and a decorative hand-painted coffered ceiling in the entryway.

Dorothy Jo loved this house. She decorated it herself and chose every piece of furniture for it. When she was terminally ill, she said, "I hope this house doesn't end up as an apartment house some day." And I am delighted to tell you, it won't. At least, not for a long, long time.

I submitted the history of this house and its features to the Los Angeles Cultural Heritage Commission and requested that it be declared an historic cultural monument. After an inspection by the commissioners, the house that Dorothy Jo loved so much and wanted protected was named historic cultural monument number 673. That means no changes without the commission's approval.

I know nothing is forever. But it's the best I can do.

• • •

As I have mentioned earlier, my involvement with animal rights has become a more important part of my life with each passing day. As proud as I may be of my nineteen Emmys and my fifty years on television, I really feel that some of the most valuable things I may do in life may be things I have yet to do. And I suspect it will be in the area of animal rights.

For instance, I have established endowment funds for the study of animal rights law at eight of the finest law schools in the country: Harvard, Columbia, Georgetown, Duke, Northwestern, UCLA, Stanford, and the University of Virginia. My thinking is that some background in animal law would be useful if, as lawyers, these graduates have cases involving animals. Of course, having studied animal law would prove to be equally valuable if they became judges.

Many, if not a majority, of the members of Congress have a legal background, and it is with legislation that we can make great strides in protecting animals. Our present federal, state, and local laws are inadequate, and frequently they are not stringently enforced. Hopefully, graduates of these eight law schools who go into politics will be inspired to introduce legislation helpful to the long-suffering animals. Incidentally, these endowment funds have not only been gratefully applauded by animal rights activists, but have been very positively reviewed by the legal community.

Since my retirement, I have established a unique endowment fund at my alma mater, Drury University, in Springfield, Missouri, for the study of animal rights. I am glad to be able to give this money to Drury because when I was there, I didn't have fifteen cents to spare. To the best of my knowledge, it is the first such endowment fund at an undergraduate school in the United States. I had the good fortune of meeting Dr. Patricia A. McEachern, who is also deeply devoted to animals. In addition to being an associate professor of French, Dr. McEachern is now director of the Drury University Forum on Animal Rights. She took on the responsibility of planning the course down to the smallest detail and carefully choosing the faculty members who will teach this interdepartmental class.

There will be six professors teaching animal ethics from a variety of angles, including religion, philosophy, environment, criminology, biology, and law. The course will count toward fulfilling ethics course requirements. It will also include seminars, conferences, and symposiums. Various animal rights experts and scholars have already been contacted, and have expressed interest and willingness to be visiting lecturers.

I am delighted to report that Dr. McEachern is already receiving inquiries from other universities and colleges that are interested in adding similar courses to their curricula.

• • •

Now that I am retired, I am devoting even more time to the DJ&T Foundation, too. When I was taping *Price,* I often spent the morning working on foundation business before I went to the studio, but now I have more time for the foundation. And I need it because the scope of the foundation is growing by leaps and bounds—of happy dogs, that is!

We have organizations receiving grants in every state in the union and multiple organizations in most states. Individuals and organizations across the country tell us that we are making a positive difference in reducing the tragic problem of animal overpopulation, and the beauty of it is that the DJ&T Foundation will go right on making a positive difference long after I am gone. Animal rights of every description are gaining momentum at a veritable tsunami rate!

Oprah Winfrey featured an exposé of puppy mills on her hugely popular television show, and the repercussions continue today. Oprah, in a matter of minutes on her show, did more to raise awareness of the puppy mill horror than anyone else thus far. Let's hear it for Oprah!

And let's hear it for Los Angeles City Councilman Richard Alarcon and Councilman Tony Cardenas! Councilman Alarcon introduced and Councilman Cardenas seconded an ordinance that requires that dogs and cats be spayed or neutered in the city of Los Angeles.

I was pleased to be able to lend a hand in getting the ordinance passed. Los Angeles is the first major city in the United States to pass such an ordinance, but officials in other cities are making inquiries, and we hope that many of them will follow suit. Already, I have had invitations to write to the mayor and council members of both Dallas and Chicago in support of spay/neuter ordinances similar to the one passed in Los Angeles.

• • •

And the animal rights tsunami rolls on to elephants—more specifically to the elephant named Maggie. You may have heard her name—Maggie's plight received worldwide attention.

While I was still doing *Price,* I received a couple of letters from Anchorage, Alaska, describing the conditions under which Maggie was living. Because of the inclement weather, Maggie had to be kept indoors seven months of the year, and an elephant cannot be healthy, let alone happy, living indoors seven months of the year. I gave the letters to Nancy Burnet of UAAR, who did her own investigation and determined that Maggie did, indeed, need our help.

For more than a year, Nancy worked with Diane Raynor and April Warwick, advising them in their Free Maggie campaign. Pat Derby and Ed Stewart, directors of the PAWS animal sanctuary near San Andreas, California, agreed to accept Maggie. An elephant is an expensive guest, but I assured Pat that it would be a pleasure for me to pick up Maggie's tab. In my opinion, the PAWS sanctuary provides the best life possible for an elephant, short of its own natural habitat, and after living all those years in Alaska under difficult conditions, Maggie deserved the best.

Moving an elephant from Alaska to California is no small chore. For transportation, I turned to Congressman Bill Young of Florida. Bill is a dear friend of mine and a great friend to animals. Maggie's plight had been well publicized, so Bill knew her story and was delighted to learn that Maggie was moving to California. He said, "Bob, I think I can get Maggie a ride."

A couple of days later, I received a telephone call from General Michael Mosley of the United States Air Force, who told me that the air force had an airplane that Maggie would fit in perfectly. It would pick her up in Anchorage and fly her to Travis Air Force Base, which is a short drive from the PAWS Sanctuary. Let me hasten to add that if you are a taxpayer, fear not. I paid the Air Force for Maggie's flight. It took all of my frequent flier miles!

Two weeks ago, Nancy Burnet and I went up to PAWS to help celebrate Ruby's first anniversary at the sanctuary. Ruby is another elephant, and Nancy and I helped get her out of the Los Angeles Zoo and into the sanctuary. Perhaps you saw me feeding Ruby some of her cake on television. After seeing Ruby roaming over acres and acres of beautiful countryside filled with trees, a pond, a mud hole—all of the things that keep elephants happy and healthy—it is easy to understand why more and more enlightened, progressive zoos are closing their elephant exhibits.

While we were at PAWS for Ruby's anniversary celebration, we visited all eleven elephants living there, including Maggie. Maggie is gaining weight and strength, and she has made friends with the other elephants. Ed Stewart pointed out that they knew she was enjoying her new home when she ripped up her first tree. Happy elephants apparently love to rip up trees. She is, of course, deeply grateful to Congressman Bill Young and General Michael Mosley of the United States Air Force.

• • •

As I come to the end of this book, I realize that there are several people who have played important roles in my life who deserve recognition. First is Joe Torrenueva, who started cutting my hair when I was hosting *Truth or Consequences* in Burbank, and is still cutting it forty-two years later. He had just begun as a hairstylist when I met him, but he later cut hair for many of Hollywood's biggest stars, including Robert Redford, Martin Sheen, Marlon Brando, Steve McQueen, Brad Pitt, Robert Wagner, and Charles Bronson. Interestingly enough, he was the stylist who gave the $400 haircut to John Edwards.

Joe didn't charge Edwards $400 for the haircut. Joe had to go to Edwards's hotel to cut his hair, and the $400 included the haircuts that Joe could have done if he had not left his salon, driven through Los Angeles traffic, cut Edwards's hair, and driven back through Los Angeles traffic to his salon. (Incidentally, these are not haircuts that we're talking about. These are hair stylings. But frankly, they'll always be haircuts to me.)

The part of this whole fiasco that I enjoyed the most was a line in the *Washington Post* that said, "Joe Torreneuva has cut them all, from Brando to Barker." I liked being in the same sentence with Brando, even if I got second billing.

My business management combo is pretty impressive, too, when it comes to longevity. Guy Gadbois, a well-known and well-respected business manager, and I were seatmates on a flight from New York City to Los Angeles in 1962. By the time the plane landed in California, I was so impressed with Guy that I retained him to handle my business affairs. Guy suggested that

I buy some land in the Perris Valley adjacent to land already purchased by two of his clients, Jimmy Stewart and Tony Curtis. I bought the land, and over the years it has become the best single investment I ever made. It may not be number one on Jimmy's and Tony's lists, but I know they did well, too.

Unfortunately, Guy passed away in 1976. But Mary Prappas had worked in Guy's office for years, and when she opened her own office, both Jimmy Stewart and I became her clients. When Mary retired in 1992, her son, William, took over the office, and both Jimmy Stewart and I became William's clients. Of course, Jimmy is gone now, but William and I are still chugging along together. In fact, William is the business manager for the DJ&T Foundation, too. So, like Tinker to Evers to Chance, it has been Guy to Mary to William for me for almost half a century.

Sol Rosenthal, a prominent entertainment attorney, and I have been associated for twenty-six years. Sol has negotiated many a contract for me professionally, and he has participated in writing the agreements for the endowment funds I have established with universities on behalf of animals.

And, of course, there is Henri Bollinger. Henri has been my public relations representative for more than twenty years. He has watched over me like a mother hen in all sorts of situations in all sorts of places with all sorts of people and never missed a beat.

Which brings me to Tom Stasinis, a true artist of the needle. Frequently, I have been complimented on my clothes, and Tom has been my tailor for thirty years. Tom has made me everything from corduroy jackets to tuxedos, and he has never dropped a stitch. He's a great luncheon companion too, with stories about clients all the way back to George Raft. (If that name isn't familiar, your grandfather will explain.)

All of these fellows with whom I have been associated for so many years are gentlemen of the old school, and I am proud to have them as friends as well as business associates.

A gentleman of the old school who is new to the Barker clan is my collaborator, Digby Diehl, with whom I have had a good time writing my book. I must also give thanks to his wife, Kay, for her proofreading and research and to his daughter Dylan, for her compliments and chocolates.

Good fortune smiled on me yet again on the day that Christina Boys became editor of *Priceless Memories*. Although Christina and I have not met, in our lengthy telephone conversations she has warmly encouraged me and expertly guided me in the preparation of this book. Working with Christina has become another one of my priceless memories.

I have a long list of cousins, nephews, a niece, and in-laws spread all over the country, but the only family I really spend any time with these days is my brother, Kent, and his wife, Beth. They live about fifteen minutes from me.

I began playing with Kent when he was a baby in his crib. He's seventy years old now, and we still enjoy playing together. But he has a couple of grandchildren now, about whom he talks endlessly. He was a lot more fun when I got to talk about me.

• • •

There's no stage manager here to give me a signal, but I think the time has come for me to wind things up. Thank you so very much for reading my book. I sincerely hope that you have enjoyed reading it even half so much as I've enjoyed writing it.

Of course, we know there's only one way for me to say the end:

This is Bob Barker reminding you to help control the pet population. Have your pets spayed or neutered.

Good-bye, everybody.

First Photo Insert

Pages 1, top; 2, bottom; 3, bottom; 4, both; 5, top two; and 8, bottom, courtesy of Ralph Edwards Productions. Pages 6, both; 7, top; 8, top; 9; and 16: *Price Is Right* and other photos courtesy of CBS Broadcasting Inc. Page 10: Originally published in the *Springfield News and Leader.* Pages 12, all; and 14, bottom left, courtesy of Tilly Barker Valandra.

Second Photo Insert

Pages 1, top; 2, 3, and 4, all; 6, top right; 7, top; 8, top and middle; 10, both; 11, bottom left; 12, top and middle; and 15, bottom: *Price Is Right* and other photos courtesy of CBS Broadcasting Inc. Page 1, middle and bottom by Bob Barker. Page 5, bottom, photos by Nelson Morris; originally published in *Service: A Publication of City Service,* July 1950. Page 9, both, courtesy of Universal Studios Licensing LLLP.